In praise of hands

In praise of hands

Contemporary Crafts of the World

Essay by Octavio Paz
Foreword by James S. Plaut
Preface by Charles F. Lombard

McClelland and Stewart Limited
in association with
the World Crafts Council
Ontario Science Centre, Toronto
Benson & Hedges (Canada) Limited

This exhibition catalogue has been prepared especially for the Ontario Science Centre exhibition IN PRAISE OF HANDS. It is available only at the exhibition (June 11-September 2, 1974).
The clothbound book is published by McClelland and Stewart Limited, 25 Hollinger Road, Toronto.

The publishers thank the National Film Board of Canada for use of still photographs from the film IN PRAISE OF HANDS, made in connection with the exhibition.

The publishers are grateful to S. Lane Faison, George Wittenborn and Company, and Presses Universitaires de France for permission to quote from and adapt the title of an essay by Henri Focillon, *Eloge de la Main* (published in the original French in *Vie des Formes,* Paris: Presses Universitaires de France, 1936, translated into English by Professor Faison under the title *In Praise of Hands* and published in *The Life of Forms in Art,* New York: Wittenborn, Schultz, Inc., 1948). "The Kizaemon Tea-bowl" is an excerpt from Sōetsu Yanagi, *The Unknown Craftsman,* adapted by Bernard Leach (Kodansha International Ltd., 10 East 53rd Street, New York, New York 10022, 1972) and is reprinted with permission of the publishers.

Library of Congress Catalog Card Number 73-89960

Published in Canada by

The Canadian Publishers
McClelland and Stewart Limited
Illustrated Books Division
25 Hollinger Road, Toronto

Designed by Joseph B. Del Valle

Manufactured in the United States of America

illustrations on preceding pages:

1 **India.** Like many Indian craftsmen, this block printer in the village of Sanganeer, Rajasthan, works on the street.

2 **Japan.** Shôji Hamada pauses while throwing a pot.

Preface

The crafts, perhaps more than any other human activity, know no boundaries; they are at the heart of every society, and reflect both man's dreams and the realities of his existence.

Craftsmen are among the most vivid recorders of today's economic, social, and religious systems, yet for too long, they, and their incredible works, have been known only to a narrow public.

Now, in this exhibition, we have for the first time the opportunity to encounter in one place the imagination and skills of contemporary craftsmen throughout the world. *In Praise of Hands* is an extraordinary panorama of handcrafted objects from over fifty countries, representing both ancient cultural traditions and personal statements in new forms and techniques.

This exhibition clearly demonstrates the fundamental contribution craftsmen of today make to our aesthetic life. Benson & Hedges (Canada) Limited is proud to offer its support. The technological revolution has brought the modern corporation into a close relationship with its environment; we know as never before that we cannot avoid the consequences of what happens around us. The artist and the craftsman make it possible for us to build the bridges of communication vital to the survival and progress of ourselves and our fellows. It is clear that if today's business is to prosper, it must look beyond the market place, become truly responsive to the needs of the people, and remain alert to the basic human values.

CHARLES F. LOMBARD
President
Benson & Hedges (Canada) Limited

This book is dedicated to Aileen Osborn Webb and Margaret Merwin Patch, two American women of courage, generosity, and vision, pioneers in befriending and supporting craftsmen everywhere, founders of the World Crafts Council.

The Kizaemon Tea-bowl

From *The Unknown Craftsman* by Sōetsu Yanagi, adapted by Bernard Leach.
Yanagi speaks of a sixteenth-century Korean bowl of the Yi dynasty.

This single Tea-bowl is considered to be the finest in the world. There are three main kinds of Tea-bowls, those originating in China, Korea and Japan, respectively. The most lovely are from Korea, and men of Tea always give them first place. . . . The finest are called *meibutsu,* signifying the particularly fine pieces. There are twenty-six bowls registered as *meibutsu,* but the finest of them all is that known as the Kizaemon *Ido.* This bowl is said to contain the essence of Tea. . . .

In 1931 I was shown this bowl in company with my friend, the potter Kanjiro Kawai. For a long time I had wished to see this Kizaemon bowl. I had expected to see that "essence of Tea," the seeing eye of Tea masters, and to test my own perception. . . . It was within box after box, five deep, buried in wool and wrapped in purple silk.

When I saw it, my heart fell. A good Tea-bowl, yes, but how ordinary! So simple, no more ordinary thing could be imagined. There is not a trace of ornament, not a trace of calculation. It is just a Korean food bowl, a bowl, moreover, that a poor man would use every day—commonest crockery.

A typical thing for his use; costing next to nothing; made by a poor man; an article without the flavor of personality; used carelessly by its owner; bought without pride; something anyone could have bought anywhere and everywhere. That is the nature of this bowl. The clay had been dug from the hill at the back of the house; the glaze was made with the ash from the hearth; the potter's wheel had been irregular. The shape revealed no particular thought: it was one of many. The work had been fast; the turning was rough, done with dirty hands; the throwing slipshod; the glaze had run over the foot. The throwing room had been dark. The thrower could not read. The kiln was a wretched affair; the firing careless. Sand had stuck to the pot, but nobody minded; no one invested the thing with any dreams. It is enough to make one give up working as a potter. . . .

This, and no more, was the truth about this, the most celebrated Tea-bowl in the land. But that was as it should be. The plain and unagitated, the uncalculated, the harmless, the straightforward, the natural, the innocent, the humble, the modest: where does beauty lie if not in these qualities? The meek, the austere, the unornate—they are the natural characteristics that gain man's affection and respect.

More than anything else, this pot is healthy. Made for a purpose, made to do work. Sold to be used in everyday life. If it were fragile, it would not serve its purpose. By its very nature, it must be robust. Its healthiness is implicit in its function. Only a commonplace practicality can guarantee health in something made.

above: 3 **Mali.** Peul woman. 4 **Panama.** Cuna Indian girl. 5 **Paraguay.** Chaco Indian woman.
below: 6 **Arab Republic of Egypt.** Bedouin woman of the Sinai. 7 **Papua New Guinea.** Woman of Sepik River District. 8 **Morocco.** Berber girl.

A World Family

This book is published on the occasion of the tenth anniversary of the World Crafts Council, founded during an international gathering of craftsmen and educators at Columbia University, New York, in 1964. During the past decade, the Council has established relations with craftsmen, and the organizations that represent their interests, on all of the world continents. Seventy-seven countries now participate in the Council's programs. Affiliation with UNESCO as a consultative nongovernmental organization has been established, and the Council has become the dominant international instrumentality for the advancement of the craftsman's welfare.

All of the objects illustrated herein have been selected by an international committee for inclusion in The First World Crafts Exhibition, being presented during the summer of 1974 at the Ontario Science Centre, Toronto. The exhibition comprises over five hundred works of craft from more than fifty countries; both the exhibition and the book offer a panorama of the world's crafts as they are practiced today in the largest metropolitan centers and the smallest, remote villages. The reader will not find in this volume an encyclopedia of world crafts or a technical manual designed to facilitate the making of crafts. Instead, like The First World Crafts Exhibition, it is a vehicle for the examination of the crafts of our time, of the social and economic conditions underlying the universal activity of craftsmen, and of the craftsman's central role in contemporary life.

Whatever their differences of origin, race, tradition, geography, or social order, the world's craftsmen have one thing—one great gift—in common. They work, create, and achieve *with their hands*. This common bond, this way of work, transcends all barriers of language and custom, making it possible for the craftsmen of the world to invent and perfect *their own* language and to communicate with each other happily and fruitfully.

If the world's craftsmen are members of one vast family, what is the family known for? How different from each other are its members? It may be said that one branch comes from the developing world, the other from the developed. One knows the mountains, the sea, the fields and forests, the life of a village. The other branch knows technology and the urban society. If the world family is thus a house divided, this is because of circumstance, not desire. Many members of the family wish to know their distant cousins better, and in so doing, to enrich their own existence.

As in all families, growth is nurtured by the sharing of learning and experience. For craftsmen everywhere, this is a constant process. Craft, like art, comes from the hand and the mind of the maker. Deftness and ingenuity emerge from the doing and re-doing, from seeing, hearing and thinking, over and over again.

Some years ago, Henri Focillon, the wise and eloquent French art historian, wrote a brilliant essay, *Eloge de la Main*. S. Lane Faison, Professor of Fine Arts at Williams College and a Focillon admirer, prepared an English translation, entitled *In Praise of Hands*. Just as Faison believed that "hands" were preferable to "the hand," *our* French edition will be entitled *Hommage aux Mains;* Focillon addressed himself to *the hand* of Rembrandt, for example, while we are concerned with *the hands* of potters, weavers, wood turners, glass blowers, and jewelers, hands working together to make something. These were Focillon's opening words:

I undertake this essay in praise of hands as if in fulfillment of a duty to a friend. Even as I begin to write, I see my own hands calling out to my mind and inciting it. Here, facing me, are these tireless companions who for so many years have served me well, one holding the paper steady, the other peopling the white page with hurried, dark, active little marks. Through his hands man establishes contact with the austerity of thought. They quarry its rough mass. Upon it they impose form, outline and, in the very act of writing, style.

The interaction of hand and mind intrigues the scientific investigator. Which is dominant? Which controls? Which gives the message, which receives and activates it?

Focillon said, "I separate hands neither from the body nor from the mind. But the relationships between mind and hand are not, however, so simple as those between a chief accustomed to obedience and a docile slave. The mind rules over the hand; hand rules over mind. . . . The hand wrenches the sense of touch away from its merely receptive passivity and organizes it for experiment and action. It teaches man to conquer space, weight, density and quantity."

The words *hand* and *craft* come together easily and naturally. Curiously enough, *craft* derives from the Teutonic *Kraft,* meaning strength or power (the power to make). Yet in post-industrial revolution German usage, crafts became *Handwerk,* or hand work. Making no longer adduced strength. The craftsman, traditionally the man of power, was reduced to a hand worker.

What, then, *is* craft? James Ackerman of Harvard, a perceptive interpreter of the arts, maintains that "the creative impulse within us takes form only through the discipline of a craft." If you ask a writer, or a painter, or a composer of music, he will often respond that the knowledge and practice of his *craft* underlies his accomplishment, that craftsmanship is essential to the creative art. Is craft therefore only technique, or is it the subtle amalgam of learning and skill that yields invention, fantasy, and art?

The craftsman, for our purposes, is a maker. He uses his hands to form, to shape, to draw in or out or to draw upon, to press, to weave and sew, to carve, to work with material, and to hold and use tools. He is at once the counterpart and antithesis of the industrial worker—counterpart because, in many industrial applications, the skills of hand are prized and necessary (as in the assembly of miniaturized electronic components); antithesis because the hand-produced object is *different* from the industrial product, differently conceived, differently made, differently used.

Twenty years ago, in *The Labyrinth of Solitude,* Octavio Paz wrote:

The modern worker lacks individuality. The class is stronger than the individual and his personality dissolves in the generic. That is the first and gravest mutilation a man suffers when he transforms himself into an industrial wage earner. Capitalism deprives him of his human nature . . . by reducing him to an element in the work process, *i.e.,* to an object. And like any object in the business world he can be bought and sold. Because of his social condition he quickly loses any concrete and human relationship to the world. The machines he operates are not his and neither are the things he produces. Actually he is not a worker at all, because he does not create individual works or is so occupied with one aspect of production that he is not conscious of those he does create.

The point is not that the *use* of man's hands has been lost in the industrial process, but that their *free* use has been lost, or worse, corrupted. In *The Unknown Craftsman,* Sōetsu Yanagi, speaking of hand and machine, said, "No machine can compare with a man's hands. Machinery gives speed, power, complete uniformity, and precision, but it cannot give creativity, adaptability, freedom, heterogeneity. These the machine is incapable of, hence the superiority of the hand, which no amount of rationalism can negate. Man prefers the creative and the free to the fixed and standardized."

The inevitable movement against technology and automation, against the dominant machine, against the dehumanization of mankind, has found its champions in the younger people of the developed countries. Their protest was at first anti-establishmentarian and nihilistic. "Dropping out" of society, the sons and daughters of affluence reacted strongly against the complacency, the institutions, the standards and the precepts of their parents. Their first motivation was rebellion, pure and simple, but from rebellion *per se* came a new and more positive notion of how life could and should be lived. Escape from the establishment led naturally to the rediscovery of life as it was lived "before technology," life *without* labor-saving devices, life *with* independence and *within* nature, life to be made more precious by one's own discoveries and the capacity to shape one's own environment. Young people have left the cities to rejoin and husband the land, to build their own dwellings, grow and raise their own food, make their own clothing, form their own utensils. Craftsmanship in all endeavors has been reasserted, newly esteemed and made vital. The industrial society's dismissal of the craftsman as a nonconformist, irrelevant eccentric has been laid to rest.

Though intent upon their new lives and the exhilarating discovery of their own hands, the curiosity of this new generation of craftsmen in Europe and North America has opened the eyes of the world to those men and women in other parts of the world who continue to make things as they always have—with their own hands, without machines and systems—things made for their own use, or their family's, or their community's. What they make still fills a broad spectrum of human need, as broad as life itself. In the pre-industrial societies of the world (which still greatly outnumber the industrial societies) the craftsman is an integral, effective member of his community, central to the social and economic system. However, because of the developing world's passion to industrialize, the village craftsman rarely enjoys the respect and status formerly accorded him. Indeed, until a substantial segment of thought and opinion began to question the values of a world grown overwhelmingly mechanized and increasingly standardized, the craftsman was in eclipse and not far from extinction.

With the rediscovery and revaluation of the crafts of the Third World, there has also come realization of the fragility of their existence. Are they an anachronism?—or do they fit into our concept of the "real world"? And if they do, *can* they or *will* they survive? In the developing countries industrialization and urbanization threaten to snuff out the feeble flame of the crafts. One knows example after example of skills lost with the passing of senior craftsmen—lost forever, because for skills handed down from generation to generation there is no longer an heir—and of villages known for their particular craft which have deteriorated or simply disappeared.

A random wanderer, traveling through an Andean village with a carload of garish plastic containers is able, inadvertently and single-handedly, to stop the production of the superb ceramic pots for which the village has been known for centuries. The village crafts are vulnerable because of the isolation and ignorance of their makers and the onslaughts made upon them by thoughtless outsiders—buyers, bureaucrats, even "reformers." Neglect has been the most corrosive factor of all.

With the resurgence of craft activity in the developed world, and the access provided to hitherto remote areas of the world by aviation, there is hardly a village anywhere that remains unvisited and unscrutinized. Many Third World governments, made newly aware of their country's richness and tradition in the crafts, are now taking preservation measures. The more sophisticated officials recognize that craftsmen are an integral element in the country's social structure; that they strengthen the work force and the level of productivity, contribute to the country's export potential, enhance tourism, and, above all, help to perpetuate the country's cultural heritage. National pride in indigenous crafts is proclaimed in advertisements and tourist brochures. Grasping the lateness of the hour, governments and private organizations are attempting to reverse the trend toward extinction.

It is doubtful that these efforts would have even commenced without stimuli from abroad; but the scene is nevertheless clouded by the continuing exploitation of the village craftsmen by those who buy his production cheap and, through successions of middlemen, bring it to a distant market at highly inflated cost. This is the greatest threat to the indigenous craftsman. No amount of cultural interest or government subsidy can insure his survival; what *can* is the provision of a living wage that enables him to continue to work as an independent craftsman.

There is a curious paradox here. Left alone, the indigenous crafts would have ceased to exist. Eventually, they may well cease to exist, perhaps within a few generations (and then the archaeologists will take over). But for the moment, at least, a spotlight has been turned on them by the well-wishing, the self-seeking, and the innocently curious. The very attention that the village craftsman receives, and the many confusing reasons for such attention, could prove in the end to be as counter-productive to his welfare as long-term neglect.

Meanwhile, in the "advanced societies," the crafts are undergoing a metamorphosis that springs naturally from the climate of doubt and anxiety that pervades their world. While they are intrigued by the primitive and the simplistic elsewhere, many craftsmen in Europe, North America, Japan and

Australasia are obsessed with the creation of new forms. Technical mastery is taken for granted, innovation is prized. Now all of the entrapments of the exhibiting artist—ego, attention, prestige—are beginning to afflict the craftsmen of New York and London and Tokyo. Having mastered *craft,* having digested tradition and found it flourishing among their brothers in less spoiled surroundings, they now reject the *concept* of craft and aspire to be known and celebrated as *artists*. The assumption is dangerous and, more than likely, self-destructive. For history tells us, directly and eloquently, that the museum object of today, revered, conserved, enveloped in glass, and protected against undue changes of temperature and humidity, is yesterday's artifact, made for use in a village far away by someone still unknown. We know that craft becomes art only in the hands of a master, and not because it is so *wished,* but because it is so *done.*

It is fascinating to contemplate the growing numbers of craftsmen working today in all media whose creativity has stretched the limits of conventional craftsmanship to attain bold solutions and new idioms of self-expression. The tendency toward distortion for distortion's sake is most apparent in the contemporary pottery of the United States and Europe. The contemporary glassmaker, *per contra,* is less likely to abandon or revile tradition, even if his efforts are technically spectacular. Weavers and workers in metal and wood have contributed exciting new dimensions, but their respect for, and their manipulation of, material remains intrinsic.

Granted that craft at the highest level of excellence becomes art, *every* object nevertheless has a function. If it is not put to some ordinary use as a container or as a utensil for eating or drinking, it is conceived to adorn, to decorate, to brighten, to embellish. It may also serve another purpose—to amuse, to comment, to provoke or titillate. What remains constant throughout the long, unbroken history of craft is the maker's *purpose* and the use for which his production is destined. In this aspect of the creative process, the craftsman fares better than the artist, who can foresee less well the fate of his work.

Many of the pieces illustrated in this volume are categorized by function—as apparel or personal adornment; as containers and utensils; as objects used to enrich the domestic environment; as the games and instruments of play and leisure; as the special tokens of ritual and ceremony; or as works intended simply to convey the *esprit,* the personal statement of the maker. All of these come within the broad range of media accepted as the craftsman's basic materials—clay, fiber, wood, glass, and metal. For it is from these materials that objects have been made since the beginning of time.

A single limitation was imposed upon the entries to The First World Crafts Exhibition—that every object submitted to the selection committee must have been produced since 1970. The exhibition and this book, therefore, provide a unique focus on the world's crafts as they are practiced *today*. The diversity of work is no more startling than the range of social, economic, and political conditions affecting its manufacture. Tradition vies with experimentation; opulence with austerity; form with formlessness; beauty with brutality; classicism with excess.

The dominant, overwhelming impact of this assemblage of the world's crafts is that it underscores the *universality* of craftsmanship. The bond of purposeful production and the common delight in the shaping of material transcend all narrower questions of geographical and social origins. In our dangerously dehumanized time the hands of man, producing the artifacts of many societies to meet an infinite number of human needs, offer some hope that man may remain the master of his world.

JAMES S. PLAUT
Secretary General
World Crafts Council

Acknowledgments

Many talents and much good will have been solicited and offered in the making of this book and the world exhibition from which it largely derives. Pride vies with humility as we seek to express our gratitude to the many generous persons and institutions whose contribution to the success of these ambitious ventures has been made so unselfishly. The national crafts organizations in the countries represented in The First World Crafts Exhibition must here be thanked collectively, for their number is large. Hundreds of crafts leaders throughout the world have probed their countries' resources diligently in order to send to Toronto those works which exemplify the present excellence of their national crafts. Many of them have also contributed invaluable assistance in the preparation of this volume. An honor roll of these organizations and individuals is presented in the appendix.

The distinguished international committee of selection, comprising Erika Billeter, Director of the Bellerive Museum, Zürich, Paul J. Smith, Director of the Museum of Contemporary Crafts, New York, and Sori Yanagi, the Tokyo industrial designer and critic, worked with authority and discernment to select the most representative objects for the exhibition and book from several thousand national submissions. Their work in the planning of these related projects is recorded with our admiration and appreciation.

The Ontario Science Centre, one of the world's newest miracles of educational innovation, has given unstintingly of its human and physical resources in the planning and making of The First World Crafts Exhibition. We are greatly indebted to the Centre's Director, Douglas N. Omand, for his wise and sensitive leadership, and to its Director of Programs, Taizo Miake, the imaginative chief architect of the exhibition. To the many other members of the Centre's staff who have rendered significant services to the World Crafts Council, notably Albert Colucci, we give our thanks for their devoted efforts and their friendship.

The Canadian Section of the World Crafts Council and its leaders have been effective entrepreneurs, linking Toronto with the world and assuming custodial responsibility for the invaluable contributions of the several Ontario and Canadian Government agencies to the enterprise. In thanking especially our Canadian directors, Joan Chalmers and Mary Eileen Hogg, we wish to honor also the splendid work of their many colleagues.

The generous grant of Benson & Hedges (Canada) Limited toward this publication and toward the enrichment of the exhibition has helped us realize these projects, and we are grateful to Nina Kaiden Wright for her initiative and guidance.

The officers, directors, and national representatives of the World Crafts Council have given constant encouragement and support to the enterprise.

Now, as to the book itself: Octavio Paz responded to our invitation to speculate on the craftsmen's role with the innate grace and sensitivity of a great poet and philosopher. We thank our friend and colleague S. Lane Faison for permitting us to put to good use once again the title "In Praise of Hands." We have enjoyed a fruitful collaboration with the New York Graphic Society through Donald Ackland, its Managing Editor, and Betty Childs, who has been a most patient and understanding editor. Joseph B. Del Valle has brought great skill and sympathy to the design.

The book would not have been achieved without the unflagging labors of the staff of the World Crafts Council. It is a joy to pay ultimate tribute to Marita Burkhart, Brooke Horgan, and Katrina Martin, and, above all, to Barbara Green and Betty Teller, who through their dedicated supervision of every element from photography to text have *lived* this book from beginning to end.

J. S. P.

9 **Norway.** A metalworker hammers a silver container at the Plus Designer-Craftsmen's Center in Frederikstad.

Contents

10 **Mexico.** Huichol Indian woman weaving with the warp attached to her feet to create tension.

Use and Contemplation

OCTAVIO PAZ

Firmly planted. Not fallen from on high: sprung up from below. Ocher, the color of burnt honey. The color of a sun buried a thousand years ago and dug up only yesterday. Fresh green and orange stripes running across its still-warm body. Circles, Greek frets: scattered traces of a lost alphabet? The belly of a woman heavy with child, the neck of a bird. If you cover and uncover its mouth with the palm of your hand, it answers you with a deep murmur, the sound of bubbling water welling up from its depths; if you tap its sides with your knuckles, it gives a tinkling laugh of little silver coins falling on stones. It has many tongues: it speaks the language of clay and minerals, of air currents flowing between canyon walls, of washerwomen as they scrub, of angry skies, of rain. A vessel of baked clay: do not put it in a glass case alongside rare precious objects. It would look quite out of place. Its beauty is related to the liquid that it contains and to the thirst that it quenches. Its beauty is corporal: I see it, I touch it, I smell it, I hear it. If it is empty, it must be filled; if it is full, it must be emptied. I take it by the shaped handle as I would take a woman by the arm, I lift it up, I tip it over a pitcher into which I pour milk or pulque—lunar liquids that open and close the doors of dawn and dark, waking and sleeping. Not an object to contemplate: an object to use.

A glass jug, a wicker basket, a coarse muslin *huipil,* a wooden serving dish: beautiful objects, not despite their usefulness but because of it. Their beauty is simply an inherent part of them, like the perfume and the color of flowers. It is inseparable from their function: they are beautiful things because they are useful things. Handcrafts belong to a world antedating the separation of the useful and the beautiful. Such a separation is more recent that is generally supposed. Many of the artifacts that find their way into our museums and private collections once belonged to that world in which beauty was

not an isolated and autonomous value. Society was divided into two great realms, the profane and the sacred. In both beauty was a subordinate quality: in the realm of the profane, it was dependent upon an object's usefulness, and in the realm of the sacred it was dependent upon an object's magic power. A utensil, a talisman, a symbol: beauty was the aura surrounding the object, the result—almost invariably an unintentional one—of the secret relation between its form and its meaning. Form: the way in which a thing is made; meaning: the purpose for which it is made.

Today all these objects, forcibly uprooted from their historical context, their specific function, and their original meaning, standing there before us in their glass display cases, strike our eye as enigmatic divinities and command our adoration. Their transfer from the cathedral, the palace, the nomad's tent, the courtesan's boudoir, and the witch's cavern to the museum was a magico-religious transmutation. Objects became icons. This idolatry began in the Renaissance and from the seventeenth century onward has been one of the religions of the West (the other being politics). Long ago, at the height of the Baroque period, Sor Juana Inés de la Cruz coined a witty little phrase poking fun at aesthetics as superstitious awe: ''A woman's hand is white and beautiful because it is made of flesh and bone, not of marble or silver; I esteem it not because it is a thing of splendor but because its grasp is firm.''

The religion of art, like the religion of politics, sprang from the ruins of Christianity. Art inherited from the religion that had gone before the power of consecrating things and imparting a sort of eternity to them: museums are our places of worship and the objects exhibited in them are beyond history; politics—or to be more precise, Revolution—meanwhile co-opted the other function of religion: changing man and society. Art was a spiritual heroism; Revolution was the building of a universal church. The mission of the artist was to transmute the object; that of the revolutionary leader was to transform human nature. Picasso and Stalin. The process has been a twofold one: in the sphere of politics, ideas were converted into ideologies and ideologies into idolatries: art objects in turn were made idols, and these idols transformed into ideas. We gaze upon works of art with the same reverent awe—though with fewer spiritual rewards—with which the sage of antiquity contemplated the starry sky above: like celestial bodies, these paintings and sculptures are pure ideas. The religion of art is a neo-Platonism that dares not confess its name—when it is not a holy war against heretics and infidels. The history of modern art may be divided into two currents: the contemplative and the combative. Such schools as Cubism and Abstract Expressionism belong to the former; movements such as Futurism, Dadaism, and Surrealism to the latter. Mystics and crusaders.

Before the aesthetic revolution the value of works of art pointed to another value. That value was the interconnection between beauty and meaning: art objects were things that were perceptual forms that in turn were signs. The meaning of a work was multiple, but all its meanings had to do with an ultimate signifier, in which meaning and being fused in an indissoluble central node: the godhead. The modern transposition: for us the artistic object is an autonomous, self-sufficient reality, and its ultimate meaning does not lie beyond the work but within it, in and of itself. It is a meaning beyond meaning: it refers to nothing whatsoever outside of itself. Like the Christian divinity, Jackson Pollock's paintings do not *mean:* they *are.*

In modern works of art meaning dissolves into the sheer emanation of being. The act of seeing is transformed into an intellectual process that is also a magic rite: to see is to understand, and to understand is to partake of the sacrament of communion. And along with the godhead and the true believers, the theologians: art critics. Their elaborate interpretations are no less abstruse than those of Medieval Scholastics and Byzantine scholars, though far less rigorously argued. The questions that Origen, Albertus Magnus, Abelard, and Saint Thomas Aquinas gravely pondered reappear in the quibbles of our art critics, though tricked out this time in fancy masquerade costumes or reduced to mere platitudes. The parallel can be extended even further: in the religion of art, we find not only divinities and their attributes and theologians who explicate them, but martyrs as well. In the twentieth century we have seen the Soviet State persecute poets and artists as mercilessly as the Dominicans extirpated the Albigensian heresy in the thirteenth.

Not unexpectedly, the exaltation and sanctification of the work of art has led to periodic rebellions and profanations. Snatching the fetish from its niche, daubing it with paint, pinning a donkey's ears and tail on it and parading it through the streets, dragging it in the mud, pinching it and proving that it is stuffed with sawdust, that it is nothing and no one and has no meaning at all—and then placing it back on its throne. The Dadaist Richard Huelsenbeck once exclaimed in a moment of exasperation: ''Art should get a sound thrashing.'' He was right —except that the welts left on the body of the Dadaist object by this scourging were like military decorations on the chests of generals: they simply enhanced its respectability. Our museums are full to bursting with anti-works of art and works of anti-art. The religion of art has been more astute than Rome: it has assimilated every schism that came along.

I do not deny that the contemplation of three sardines on a plate or of one triangle and one rectangle can enrich us spiritually; I merely maintain that the repetition of this act soon degenerates into a boring ritual. For that very reason the Futurists, confronted with the neo-Platonism of the Cubists, urged a return to art with a message. The Futurists' reaction was a healthy one, but at the same time an ingenuous one. Being more perspicacious, the Surrealists insisted that the work of art should say something. Since they realized that it would be foolish to reduce the work of art to its content or its message, they resorted to a notion that Freud had made common currency: that of *latent content.* What the work of art says is not be to found in its manifest content, but rather in what it says without actually saying it: what is behind the forms, the colors, the words. This was a way of loosening the theological knot binding being and meaning together without undoing it altogether, so as to preserve, to the maximum extent possible, the ambiguous relation between the two terms.

The most radical of the avant-gardists was Marcel Duchamp: the work of art passes by way of the senses but its real goal lies farther on. It is not a thing: it is a fan of signs that as it opens and closes alternately reveals its meaning to us and conceals it from us. The work of art is an intelligible signal beamed back and forth between meaning and non-meaning. The danger of this approach—a danger that Duchamp did not always manage to avoid—is that it may lead too far in the opposite direction, leaving the artist with the concept and without the object, with the *trouvaille* and without the *thing*. This is the fate that has befallen his imitators. It should also be said that frequently they are left both without the object and without the concept. It scarcely bears repeating that art is not a concept: art is a thing of the senses. Speculation centered on a pseudo-concept is even more boring than contemplation of a still-life. The modern religion of art continually circles back upon itself without ever finding the path to salvation: it keeps shifting back and forth from the negation of meaning for the sake of the object to the negation of the object for the sake of meaning.

The industrial revolution was the other side of the coin of the artistic revolution. The ever-increasing production of ever-more-perfect, identical objects was the precise counterpart of the consecration of the work of art as a unique object. As our museums became crowded with art objects, our houses became filled with ingenious gadgets. Precise, obedient, mute, anonymous instruments. But it would be wrong to call them ugly. In the early days of the industrial revolution aesthetic considerations scarcely played any role at all in the production of useful objects. Or better put, these considerations produced results quite different from what manufacturers had expected. It is superimposition that is responsible for the ugliness of many objects dating from the prehistory of industrial design—an ugliness not without a certain charm: the "artistic" element, generally borrowed from the academic art of the period, is simply "added onto" the object properly speaking. The results were not always displeasing. Many of these objects —I am thinking in particular of those of the Victorian era and those in the so-called "Modern Style"—belong to the same family of mermaids and sphinxes. A family ruled by what might be called the aesthetics of incongruity. In general the evolution of the industrial object for everyday use followed that of artistic styles. It was almost always a borrowing—sometimes a caricature, sometimes a felicitous copy—from the most fashionable artistic trend of the moment. Industrial design consistently lagged behind the art of the period, and imitated artistic styles only after they had lost their initial freshness and were about to become aesthetic clichés.

Modern design has taken other paths—its own characteristic ones—in its search for a compromise between usefulness and aesthetics. At times it has achieved a successful compromise, but the result has been paradoxical. The aesthetic ideal of functional art is to increase the usefulness of the object in direct proportion to the amount by which its materiality can be decreased. The simplification of forms and the way in which they function becomes the formula: the maximum efficiency is to be achieved by the minimum of presence. An aesthetic mindful of the realm of mathematics, where the *elegance* of an equation is a function of the simplicity of its formulation and the inevitability of its solution. The ideal of modern design is invisibility: the less visible functional objects are, the more beautiful they are. A curious transposition of fairy tales and Arabic legends to a world governed by science and the notions of usefulness and efficiency: the designer dreams of objects which, like *jinni,* are mute and intangible servants. The precise opposite of craftwork: a physical presence which enters us by way of the senses and in which the principle of maximum utility is continually violated in favor of tradition, imagination, and even sheer caprice. The beauty of industrial design is conceptual in nature: if it expresses anything at all, it is the precise accuracy of a formula. It is the sign of a function. Its rationality confines it to one and only one alternative: either an object will work or it won't. In the second case it must be thrown into the trash barrel. It is not simply its usefulness that makes the handcrafted object so captivating. It lives in intimate connivance with our senses and that is why it is so difficult to part company with it. It is like throwing an old friend out into the street.

There comes a moment, however, when the industrial object finally turns into a presence with an aesthetic value: when it becomes useless. It is then transformed into a symbol or an emblem. The locomotive that Whitman sings of is a machine that has stopped running and no longer propels trainloads of passengers or freight: it is a motionless monument to speed. Whitman's disciples—Valéry Larbaud and the Italian Futurists— were sent into ecstasies by the beauty of locomotives and railroad tracks at precisely the point in time when other means of transportation—the airplane, the automobile—were beginning to replace the train. The locomotives of these poets are the equivalent of the fake ruins of the eighteenth century: they complement the landscape. The cult of the mechanical is nature-worship turned topsy-turvy: usefulness that is becoming useless beauty, an organ without a function. Through ruins

11 **Ghana.** Craftsmen in Anhiniaa making ceremonial stools.

history again becomes an integral part of nature, whether we are contemplating the crumbled stone walls of Ninevah or a locomotive graveyard in Pennsylvania.

This affection of machines and contraptions that have fallen into disuse is not simply another proof of the incurable nostalgia that man feels for the past. It also reveals a blind spot in the modern sensibility: our inability to interrelate beauty and usefulness. Two things stand in our way: the religion of art forbids us to regard the useful as beautiful; the worship of usefulness leads us to conceive of beauty not as a presence but as a function. This may well be the reason for the extraordinary poverty of technology as a source of myths: aviation is the realization of an age-old dream that appears in every society, yet it has failed to create figures comparable to Icarus and Phaeton.

The industrial object tends to disappear as a form and to become indistinguishable from its function. Its being is its meaning and its meaning is to be useful. It is the diametrical opposite of the work of art. Craftwork is a mediation between these two poles: its forms are not governed by the principle of efficiency but of pleasure, which is always wasteful, and for which no rules exist. The industrial object allows the superfluous no place; craftwork delights in decoration. Its predilection for ornamentation is a violation of the principle of efficiency. The decorative patterns of the handcrafted object generally have no function whatsoever; hence they are ruthlessly eliminated by the industrial designer. The persistence and the proliferation of purely decorative motifs in craftwork reveal to us an intermediate zone between usefulness and aesthetic contemplation. In the work of handcraftsmen there is a constant shifting back and forth between usefulness and beauty. This continual interchange has a name: pleasure. Things are pleasing because they are useful *and* beautiful. This copulative conjunction defines craftwork, just as the disjunctive conjunction defines art and technology: usefulness *or* beauty. The handcrafted object satisfies a need no less imperative than hunger and thirst: the need to take delight in the things that we see and touch, whatever their everyday uses may be. This necessity is not reducible either to the mathematical ideal that acts as the norm for industrial design or to the strict rites of he religion of art. The pleasure that craftwork gives us is a twofold transgression: against the cult of usefulness and against the cult of art.

Since it is a thing made by human hands, the craft object preserves the fingerprints—be they real or metaphorical—of the artisan who fashioned it. These imprints are not the signature of the artist; they are not a name. Nor are they a trademark. Rather, they are a sign: the scarcely visible, faded scar commemorating the original brotherhood of men and their separation. Being made *by* human hands, the craft object is made *for* human hands: we can not only see it but caress it with our fingers. We look at the work of art but we do not touch it. The religious taboo that forbids us to touch the statues of saints on an altar—"You'll burn your hands if you touch the Holy Tabernacle," we were told as children—also applies to paintings and sculptures. Our relation to the industrial object is functional; to the work of art, semi-religious; to the handcrafted object, corporal. The latter in fact is not a relation but a contact. The trans-personal nature of craftwork is expressed, directly and immediately, in sensation: the body is participation. To feel is first of all to be aware of something or someone not ourselves. And above all else: to feel *with* someone. To be able to feel itself, the body searches for another body. We feel *through* others. The physical, bodily ties that bind us to others are no less strong than the legal, economic, and religious ties that unite us. The handmade object is a sign that expresses human society in a way all its own: not as work (technology), not as symbol (art, religion), but as a mutually shared physical life.

The pitcher of water or wine in the center of the table is a point of confluence, a little sun that makes all those gathered together one. But this pitcher that serves to quench the thirst of all of us can also be transformed into a flower vase by my wife. A personal sensibility and fantasy divert the object from its usual function and shift its meaning: it is no longer a vessel used for containing a liquid but one for displaying a carnation. A diversion and a shift that connect the object with another region of human sensibility: imagination. This imagination is social: the carnation in the pitcher is also a metaphorical sun shared with everyone. In fiestas and celebrations the social radiation of the object is even more intense and all-embracing. In the fiesta a collectivity partakes of communion with itself and this communion takes place by way of ritual objects that almost invariably are handcrafted objects. If the fiesta is shared participation in primordial time—the collectivity literally shares among its members, like bread that has been blessed, the date being commemorated—handcraftsmanship is a sort of fiesta of the object: it transforms the everyday utensil into a sign of participation.

In bygone days, the artist was eager to be like his masters, to be worthy of them through his careful imitation of them. The modern artist wants to be different, and his homage to tradition takes the form of denying it. If he seeks a tradition, he searches for one somewhere outside the West, in the art of primitive peoples or in that of other civilizations. Because they are negations of the Western tradition, the archaic quality of primitive craftsmanship or the antiquity of the Sumerian or Mayan object are, paradoxically, forms of novelty. The aesthetic of constant change demands that each work be new and totally different from those that have preceded it; and at the same time novelty implies the negation of the tradition closest at hand. Tradition is thus converted into a series of sharp breaks. The frenetic search for change also governs industrial production, though for different reasons: each new object, the result of a new process, drives off the market the object that has immediately preceded it. The history of craftwork, however, is not a succession of new inventions or of unique (or supposedly unique) new objects. In point of fact, craftwork has no history, if we view history as an uninterrupted series of changes. There is no sharp break, but rather continuity, between its past and its present. The modern artist has set out to conquer eternity, and the designer to conquer the future; the craftsman allows himself to be conquered by time. Traditional yet not historical, intimately linked to the past but not precisely datable, the handcrafted object refutes the mirages of history and the illusions of the future. The craftsman does not seek to win a victory over time, but to become one with its flow. By way of repetitions in the form of variations at once imperceptible and genuine, his works become part of an enduring tradition. And in so doing, they long outlive the up-to-date object that is the "latest thing."

Industrial deisgn tends to be impersonal. It is subservient to the tyranny of function and its beauty lies in this subservience. But only in geometry is functional beauty completely realized, and only in this realm are truth and beauty one and the same thing; in the arts properly speaking, beauty is born of a necessary violation of norms. Beauty—or better put: art—is a violation of functionality. The sum total of these transgressions constitutes what we call a style. If he followed his own logical principles to the limit, the designer's ideal would be the absence of any style whatsoever: forms reduced to their function, as the artist's style would be one that began and ended in each of his works. (Perhaps that is the goal that Mallarmé and Joyce set for themselves.) The one difficulty is that no work of art is its own beginning and its own end. Each is a language at once personal and collective: a style, a manner. Styles are a reflection of communal experiences, and every true work of art is both a departure from and a confirmation of the style of its own time and place. By violating that style, the work realizes all the potentialities of the latter. Craftwork, once again, lies squarely beween these two poles: like industrial design, it is anonymous; like the work of art, it is a style. By comparison with industrial designs, however, the handcrafted object is anonymous but not impersonal; by comparison with the work of art, it emphasizes the collective nature of style and demonstrates to us that the prideful *I* of the artist is a *we*.

Technology is international. Its achievements, its methods, and its products are the same in every corner of the globe. By suppressing national and regional particularities and peculiarities, it has impoverished the world. Having spread from one end of the earth to the other, technology has become the most powerful agent of historical entropy. Its negative consequences can be summed up in one succinct phrase: it imposes uniformity without furthering unity. It levels the differences between distinctive national cultures and styles, but it fails to eradicate the rivalries and hatreds between peoples and States. After turning rivals into identical twins, it purveys the very same weapons to both. What is more, the danger of technology lies not only in the death-dealing power of many of its inventions but in the fact that it constitutes a grave threat to the very essence of the historical process. By doing away with the diversity of societies and cultures it does away with history itself. The marvelous variety of different societies is the real creator of history: encounters and conjunctions of dissimilar groups and cultures with widely divergent techniques and ideas. The historical process is undoubtedly analogous to the twofold phenomenon that geneticists call *inbreeding* and *outbreeding,* and anthropologists *endogamy* and *exogamy*. The great world civilizations have been syntheses of different and diametrically opposed cultures. When a civilization has not been exposed to the threat and the stimulus of another civilization—as was the case with pre-Columbian America down to the sixteenth century—it is fated to mark time and wander round and round in circles. The experience of the *Other* is the secret of change. And of life as well.

Modern technology has brought about numerous and profound transformations. All of them, however, have had the same goal and the same import: the extirpation of the *Other*. By leaving the aggressive drives of humans intact and reducing all mankind to uniformity, it has strengthened the forces working toward the extinction of humanity. Craftwork, by contrast, is not even national: it is local. Indifferent to boundaries and systems of government, it has survived both republics and empires: the art of making the pottery, the woven baskets, and the musical instruments depicted in the frescoes of Bonampak has survived Mayan high priests, Aztec warriors, Spanish friars, and Mexican presidents. These arts will also survive Yankee tourists. Craftsmen have no fatherland: their real roots are in their native village—or even in just one quarter of it, or within their own families. Craftsmen defend us from the artificial uniformity of technology and its geometrical wastelands: by preserving differences, they preserve the fecundity of history.

The craftsman does not define himself either in terms of his nationality or of his religion. He is not faithful to an idea, nor yet to an image, but to a practical discipline: his craft. His workshop is a social microcosm governed by its own special laws. His workday is not rigidly laid out for him by a time clock, but by a rhythm that has more to do with the body and its sensitivities than with the abstract necessities of producion. As he works, he can talk with others and may even burst into song. His boss is not an invisible executive, but a man advanced in years who is his revered master and almost always a relative, or at least a close neighbor. It is revealing to note that despite its markedly collectivist nature, the craftsman's workshop has never served as a model for any of the great utopias of the West. From Tommaso Campanella's *Civitas Solis* to Charles Fourier's phalansteries and on down to the Communist collectives of the industrial era, the prototypes of the perfect social man have never been craftsmen but priest-sages and gardener-philosophers and the universal worker in whom daily praxis and scientific knowledge are conjoined. I am naturally not maintaining that craftsmen's workshops are the very image of perfection. But I do believe that, precisely because of their imperfection, they can point to a way as to how we might

humanize our society: their imperfection is that of men, not of systems. Because of its physical size and the number of people constituting it, a community of craftsmen favors democratic ways of living together; its organization is hierarchical but not authoritarian, being a hierarchy based not on power but on degrees of skill: masters, journeymen, apprentices; and finally, craftwork is labor that leaves room both for carefree diversion and for creativity. After having taught us a lesson in sensibility and the free play of the imagination, craftwork also teaches us a lesson in social organization.

Until only a few short years ago, it was generally thought that handcrafts were doomed to disappear and be replaced by industrial production. Today however, precisely the contrary is occurring: handmade artifacts are now playing an appreciable role in world trade. Handcrafted objects from Afghanistan and Sudan are being sold in the same department stores as the latest products from the design studios in Italian or Japanese factories. This rebirth is particularly noticeable in the highly industrialized countries, affecting producer and consumer alike. Where industrial concentration is heaviest—as in Massachusetts, for instance—we are witnessing the resurrection of such time-hallowed trades as pottery making, carpentry, glass blowing. Many young people of both sexes who are fed up with and disgusted by modern society have returned to craftwork. And even in the underdeveloped countries, possessed by the fanatical (and untimely) desire to become industrialized as rapidly as possible, handcraft traditions have undergone a great revival recently. In many of these countries, the government itself is actively encouraging handcraft production. This phenomenon is somewhat disturbing, since government support is usually inspired by commercial considerations. The artisans who today are the object of the paternalism of official state planners were yesterday threatened by the projects for "modernization" dreamed up by the same bureaucrats, intoxicated by economic theories they have picked up in Moscow, London, or New York. Bureaucracies are the natural enemy of the craftsman, and each time that they attempt to "guide" him, they corrupt his sensibility, mutilate his imagination, and debase his handiwork.

The return to handcraftsmanship in the United States and in Western Europe is one of the symptoms of the great change that is taking place in our contemporary sensibility. We are confronting in this case yet another expression of the rebellion against the abstract religion of progress and the quantitative vision of man and nature. Admittedly, in order to feel disillusioned by progress, people must first have undergone the experience of progress. It is hardly likely that the under-developed countries have yet reached the point of sharing this disillusionment, even though the disastrous consequences of industrial super-productivity are becoming more and more evident. We learn only with our own thinking-caps, not other people's. Nonetheless, how can anyone fail to see where the faith in limitless progress has led? If every civilization ends in a heap of rubble—a jumble of broken statues, toppled columns, indecipherable graffiti—the ruins of industrial society are doubly impressive: because they are so enormous in scope and because they are so premature. Our ruins are beginning to overshadow our constructions, and are threatening to bury us alive. Hence the popularity of handcrafts is a sign of health—like the return to Thoreau and Blake, or the rediscovery of Fourier. Our senses, our instincts, our imagination always range far ahead of our reason. The critique of our civilization began with the Romantic poets, just as the industrial era was dawning. The poetry of the twentieth century carried on the Romantic revolt and rooted it even more deeply, but only very recently has this spiritual rebellion penetrated the minds and hearts of the vast majority of people. Modern society is beginning to question the principles that served as its cornerstone two centuries ago, and is searching for other paths. We can only hope that it is not too late.

The destiny of the work of art is the air-conditioned eternity of the museum; the destiny of the industrial object is the trash barrel. The handcrafted object ordinarily escapes the museum and its glass display cases, and when it does happen to end up in one, it acquits itself honorably. It is not a unique object, merely a typical one. It is a captive example, not an idol. Handcrafted artifacts do not march in lockstep with time, nor do they attempt to overcome it. Experts periodically examine the inroads that death is making in works of art: cracks in paintings, fading outlines, changes in color, the leprosy eating away both the frescoes of Ajanta and Leonardo da Vinci's canvases. The work of art, as a material thing, is not eternal. And as an idea? Ideas too grow old and die. The work of art is not eternal. But artists often forget that their work is the possessor of the secret of the only real time: not an empty eternity but the sparkling instant, and the capacity to quicken the spirit and reappear, even if only as a negation, in the works that are its descendants. For the industrial object no resurrection is possible: it disappears as rapidly as it first appeared. If it left no trace at all, it would be truly perfect; unfortunately, it has a body and once that body has ceased to be useful, it becomes mere refuse that is difficult to dispose of. The obscene indestructibility of trash is no less pathetic than the false eternity of the museum.

The thing that is handmade has no desire to last for thousands upon thousands of years, nor is it possessed by a frantic drive to die an early death. It follows the appointed round of days, it drifts with us as the current carries us along together, it wears away little by little, it neither seeks death nor denies it: it accepts it. Between the timeless time of the museum and the speeded-up time of technology, craftsmanship is the heartbeat of human time. A thing that is handmade is a useful object but also one that is beautiful; an object that lasts a long time but also one that slowly ages away and is resigned to so doing; an object that is not unique like the work of art and can be replaced by another object that is similar but not identical. The craftsman's handiwork teaches us to die and hence teaches us to live.

Cambridge, Massachusetts
December 7, 1973

Translated from the Spanish by Helen R. Lane

The Crafts and the Makers

Apparel and Adornment

The instinct to adorn the body is evidently as old as the necessity to protect it. Cosmetics were artfully used by the ancient Egyptians, and jewelry of great elaboration and delicacy has been taken from many early tombs. Although most clothing and adornments were made by the wearer himself, special skills required for such articles as shoes and jewelry led early in history to the development of occupations based on providing articles for others. Jewelers and weavers are mentioned in the Bible, and the clothiers' guilds were important in the commerce of medieval Europe. Historically, the manufacture of clothing has been a mainstay of commerce.

Until the industrial revolution, virtually all clothing was made from materials woven, cut, assembled and stitched by hand. Today most articles are mass-produced, but even now single elements are likely to be made by hand—a cap, a scarf, a necklace, a sweater, a belt. In both the developing and the developed countries, there is an immense army of craftsmen producing an endless variety of articles of apparel and adornment. The range is inexhaustible, for throughout the world there are knitters, weavers, and jewelers, and craftsmen fashioning beads, feathers, and all manner of things. They serve themselves, or their villages, or the unknown consumer.

Fashion seems to have existed as long as mankind itself, for it is based upon the aspiration to separate oneself from one's peers by *appearing* to be different, and upon the innate desire for colors and forms to dispel the monotony of existence. Today, the value placed on self-expression has given impetus to the making of one's own clothing, or at least those accents of personal appearance that contribute to the illusion of individualism. Fashion and costume are said to be only skin-deep; nevertheless, they reveal in large measure the individual psyche.

12 **India,** Khadavan, Maharashtra. Sandals,
wood with hide straps (length 28 cm).
Such wooden sandals, originally made
with bark straps, have traditionally been
used for the purification bath before
worship.

below:

13 **Nepal.** Tsetten Pema Wongchuk,
Tibetan refugee. Boots (*zompa*, Sherpa
boots), embroidered cloth and yak
leather (length 28.5 cm). This typical
boot of the Tibetan plateau region has
been in use since the seventh century.
Its design is well suited for walking
on snow and in mountainous country.

14 **Mexico,** Oaxaca. Trique Indian.
Woman's dress *(huipil),* wild cotton
woven on backstrap loom, natural dyes
from local plants. The huipil, of
pre-Columbian origin, is still worn by
the women of this region and made by
them using the ancient methods. The
principal motif appears on the central
section just below the neck. Ribbons
cover the seams joining the three
sections of the garment.

15 **India.** Sari-clad women tying bunches in white cloth in preparation for tie-dyeing.

16 **India,** Kanchipuram, Madras. Sari, handwoven silk and gold thread (550 x 115 cm). Detail.

17 **Mali.** Peul weaver. Strip weaving, the most common weaving technique in West Africa, is generally done by men. The narrow strips are sewn together vertically to make robes and coverlets.

18 **Ghana.** Ashanti tribesman wearing ceremonial dress of *adinkra* cloth.

below:

19 **Ghana.** Osei Kwabena, Ashanti tribe. *Adinkra* cloth, embroidered and hand-stamped cotton (342 x 230 cm). Detail. Men wear this traditional fabric on special occasions. Its name is derived from the adinkra motifs hand stamped on the cloth, each of which has a meaning. The design repeated here in the upper left, center, and lower right represents *"Dwanimen"* (ram's horns) and means, "The strength of the ram lies in its horns: once they are plucked off it is finished." To make adinkra cloth, a craftsman tears a piece of undecorated material into regular strips and joins them with embroidery; the adinkra craftsman then stamps the cloth, using carved gourd stamps and bark dye.

31

20 **Ghana.** M. K. Mensah, Ashanti tribe.
Kente cloth, cotton, handwoven in
strips and sewn together (327 x 213
cm). Detail. Kente originated in the
Ashanti kingdom about three hundred
years ago. The ceremonial figurative
designs are often woven in silk in
special motifs for the Asantehene
(ruler) and chiefs. Less elaborate
examples made of rayon or cotton are
worn by tribesmen to add color and
pomp to special occasions.
Lent by Daniel Cobblah, Accra, Ghana.

opposite:

21 **Japan.** Keisuke Serizawa. Costume,
flax, woven and stencil dyed (length
137 cm).

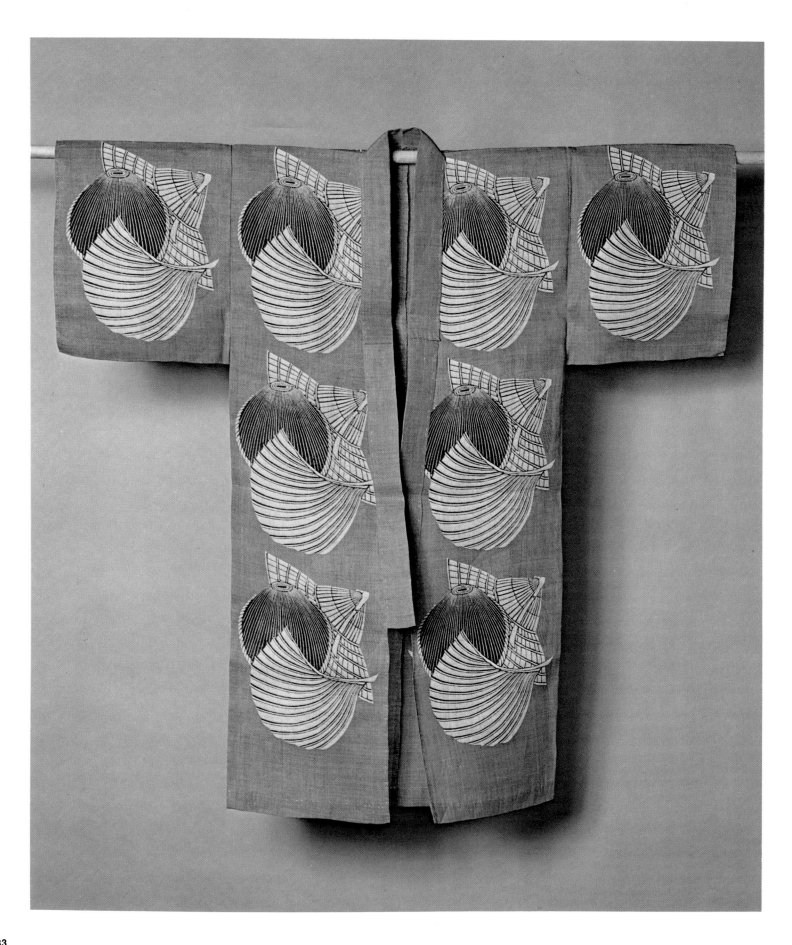

25 **Malta.** Gozo Handicrafts. Jacket,
crocheted spun and unspun sheep's
wool (length 76 cm).

opposite:

26 **Spain,** Galicia. Raincoat, straw, twining
(length 120 cm). Coats of this type are
used by shepherds in the mountains of
Galicia, near the Portuguese border.

27 **Bolivia,** Chuquisaca. Indians of
Tarabuco village. Purses (*chuspas*),
woven sheep's wool (each 16 x 16 cm).
These purses are similar in pattern,
shape, and size to those found in the
graves of wealthy Incas. They are worn
only by men, who use them to carry the
coca leaves they chew; they were
probably used for the same purpose
during the Inca period.

opposite:

28 **Papua New Guinea,** East Sepik District.
Bag, netted bark fiber mounted with
tail feathers of great black cockatoo and
sulphur-crested cockatoo (width 60 cm).

29 **Cameroon.** Bamun tribe. Chief's hat, knotted fiber, dyed feathers and porcupine quills (seen closed *below*). When the knotted cap is pulled down over the skull, this "basket" of feathers opens into a ceremonial hat (*right;* diameter opened 42 cm).

opposite:

30 **Papua New Guinea,** Eastern Highlands. Dance headdress, cassowary feathers, parrot plumes, and shells (height 48 cm).

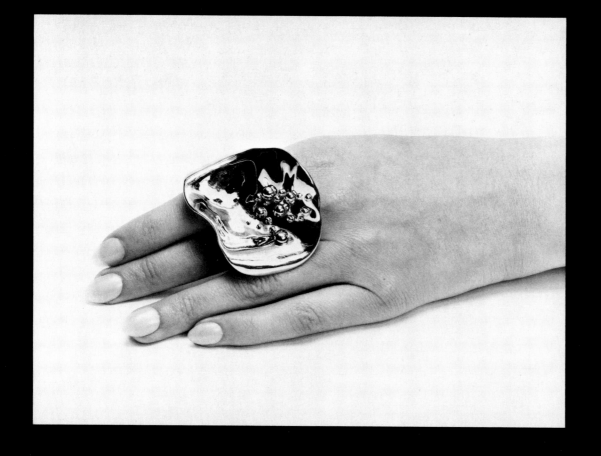

above:

34 **Jordan.** Ibrahim Yousef. Necklace, old
coins and amber (length 56 cm).
Detail. Coins are commonly used for
adornment in the Middle East.

35 **Israel.** Moshe Ben-David. Silver
pendant with turquoise on necklace
of silver and carnelian beads (pendant:
4 x 8 cm). The women of the desert
wear this type of pendant, which
contains a script for protection against
the evil eye, as a good luck charm.
The design is influenced by traditional
Yemenite motifs.

36 **Netherlands.** Chris Steenbergen.
Bracelet, gold (diameter 10 cm).

37 **Ethiopia.** Bracelets, silver (diameter
5.5 cm).

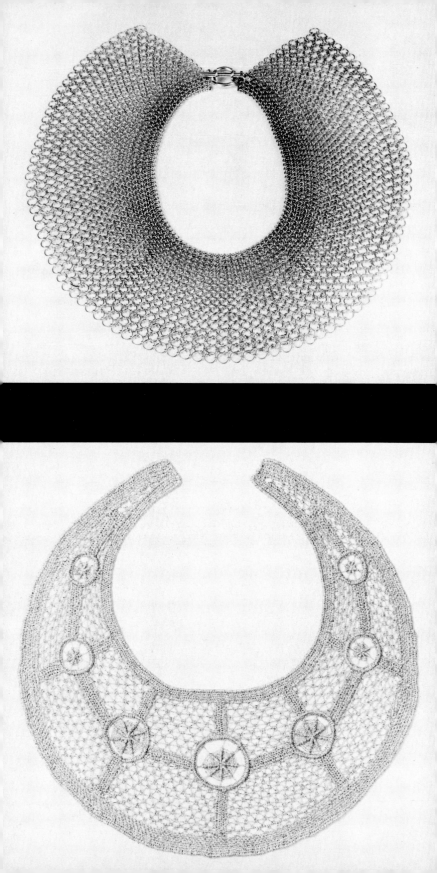

left:
40 **Norway.** Rolf Grude. Necklace with pendant, knitted sterling silver thread with rutilated quartz bead (length 14 cm).

below:
41 **Netherlands.** Gijs Bakker. Necklace, anodized aluminum, cut from blue aluminum tube (25 x 15 cm).

opposite, above:
38 **Denmark.** Peder Musse. *Chain Mail,* sterling silver necklace (diameter 40 cm). This piece was inspired by medieval ring mail and the large lace collars of the Renaissance.

opposite, below:
39 **Ireland.** Sister Rosaleen McCabe. *Lismore,* needlepoint lace collar, gold lurex yarn worked in Kenmare buttonhole stitch (maximum width 30 cm). This is an adaptation in lace work of the traditional metal collars which have a long tradition in Ireland. The design is based on the head of the Lismore Crozier (bishop's staff), which dates from the early twelfth century.

42 **United Kingdom.** Susanna Heron. *Greens and Blues,* bracelet, silver inlaid with resin (outside diameter 11 cm). *Lent by The Royal Scottish Museum, Edinburgh.*

43 **Denmark.** Ellen M. Brøker. Bracelet, sterling silver and wolf fur (diameter 24 cm).

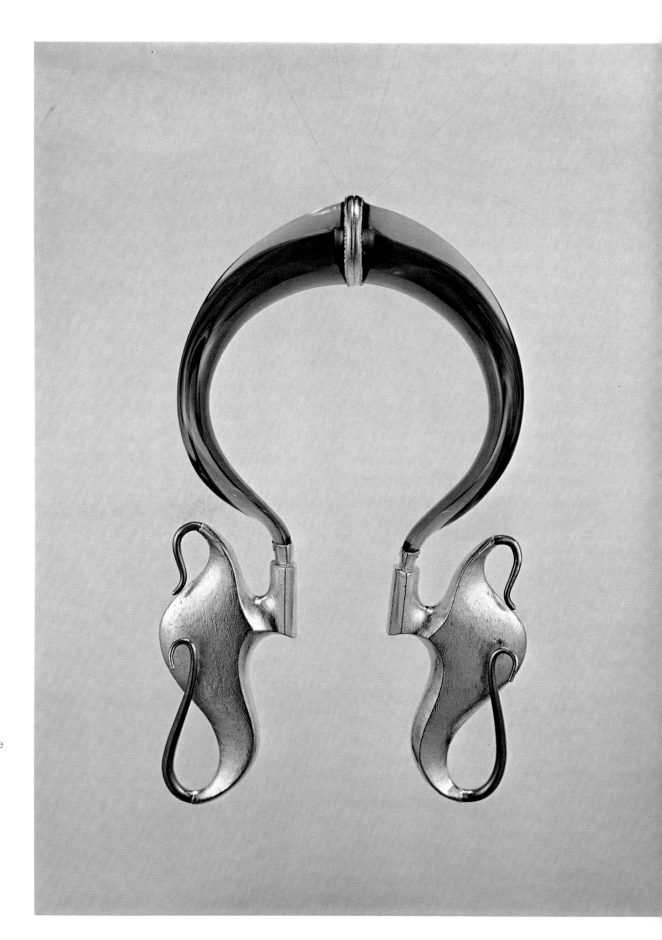

44 **United States.** Stanley Lechtzin. *Torque #33 D,* body decoration, cast polyester, electroformed silver, silver gilt (length 30 cm). "I attempt to create personal values using materials and processes which today are used in a mechanical and anonymous manner by industry. The control I exercise over the metal as it grows in the electrolytic solution is analagous to growth processes observed in nature. It brings to mind crystal growth, the growth of coral under the sea, and the multiplication of simple organisms under the microscope."

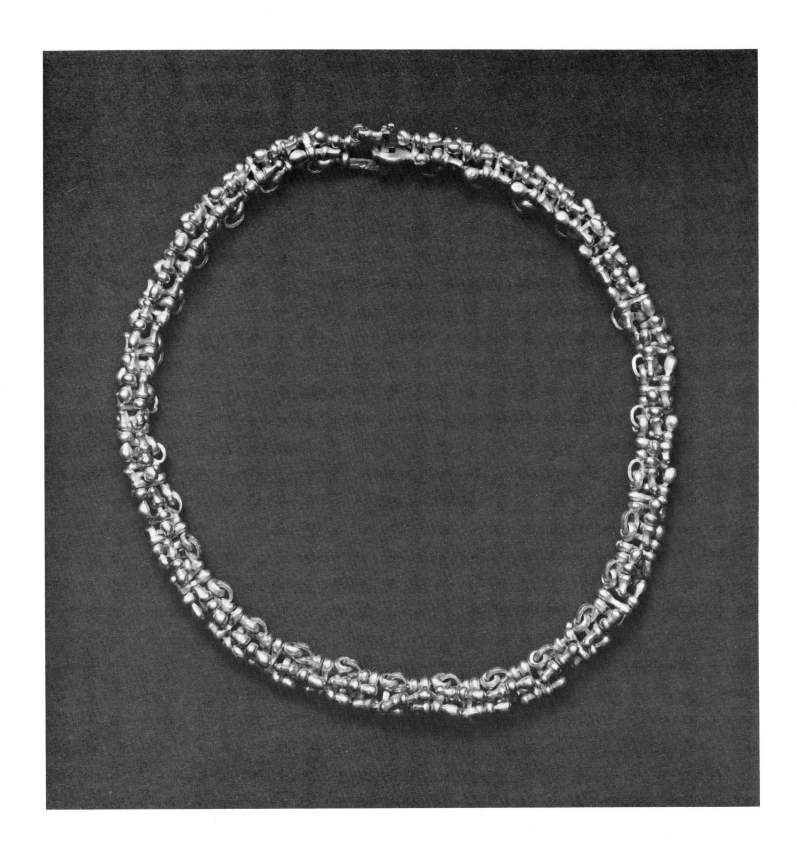

45 **Germany.** Wolfgang Skoluda. Neck
chain, gold (length 36 cm).

left:

46   **Papua New Guinea,** Madang District. Armband, natural-dyed plant fibers decorated with shells (circumference 37 cm). This band is worn on the upper arm during dances and festivals.

47   **New Hebrides,** Melsissi village, Pentecost Island. Combs, wood and hemp cord, woven (length 18 cm).

opposite, above:

48   **Colombia,** Cauca region. Hat, carob leaves sewn with vegetable fiber (diameter 55 cm). These waterproof hats, worn by the inhabitants of Guapí on the Pacific coast, are sewn when the leaves are wet.

opposite, below:

49   **Venezuela.** Sigala. Wedding crown, silver and pearls (height 11.5 cm). This crown was designed for the wedding of the craftsman's sister.

above:

50   **Peru,** Santiago de Pupuja, Puno. Bowler hats, hand-pressed wool felt, embroidery (diameter 30 cm). The bowler is said to have become popular in this region when the railroad was being built from Arequipa to Puno about one hundred years ago.

The Home: Utility and Embellishment

Domus, the home, the hearth, the center of life since man emerged from the cave, has always provided a natural focus for craftsmanship. The building of shelter has always been complemented by man's urge to fashion articles for his everyday use and for the enrichment of his surroundings. Tomb excavations have yielded a vast array of artifacts, documenting dramatically the cooking, eating, drinking, storing, seating, and sleeping customs of ancient peoples: vessels of clay and metal; chairs of wood, bone, and cane; wicker tables; corded beds; wooden and stone headrests; wooden chests; baskets; linen coverlets; metal tools; mats of woven rushes—all of these have come down to us excellently preserved and in great profusion.

The interiors of Egyptian, Greek, and Roman houses were furnished stylishly and with careful attention to colors, patterns, and textures. Decorative objects in precious metals and glass, and in brilliant hues, enlivened the homes of the ruling classes. Indeed, the opulence of the home, from Roman emperor to latterday tycoon, has reflected accurately the owner's wealth and material resources. The contents of chateaux, palazzi, and stately homes have provided the most tangible and enduring evidence of the taste, learning, and power of Europe's leaders for fifteen hundred years; and as waves of European influence have engulfed the Americas from the sixteenth century onwards, interior style has been the handmaiden of each successive architectural mode.

In this century all of the world's cultures have become intermingled in the articulation of designs for living. The stern architectural doctrines of the Bauhaus and of the International Style, dominated by Le Corbusier and Mies van der Rohe, led the home planner in Western societies into a period of geometric frugality; but in recent years the colorful and exotic materials of Africa, Asia, and Latin America have contributed vivid counterpoints to this persistently austere theme. The uniquely lovely form of the Japanese house, with its insistence upon selectivity of materials and accoutrements, has also had a profound effect upon the course of Western design. The present generation of home planners tends to avoid doctrinaire solutions and to insist that, just as man's home is his castle, man should create his own environment. If there is today some negation of the home as such, there is also a fresh emphasis upon individuality and freedom of choice. The home may well be said to be returning to its earliest function as a workable entity and a natural vehicle for the expression of man's best impulses.

51 **Poland.** Ladle, carved wood (length 30.5 cm).

opposite, above:

52 **Poland.** A woven house decorated with typical Polish flower designs.

opposite, below:

53 **Poland.** The oven is the center of this kitchen; the caged area in its base is a hutch for rabbits or chickens. The tree stump in the foreground serves as a chopping block.

Containers and Utensils

opposite:

54 **Ethiopia,** Bale province. Milk container with lid, carved wood, woven basketry, leather (height 65 cm). The basketry of this piece is blackened from smoke, as it is a common practice in parts of Ethiopia and northern Kenya to burn small pieces of wood inside the containers to give a smoky flavor to the milk.

55 **Ethiopia,** Harrarge province. *Injera* table basket with lid, woven straw and grasses (height 82 cm). Injera, the flat, round native bread, is arranged with its accompanying sauces in the shallow top. The open basket is used as a table, the Ethiopians sitting around it and eating the injera with their fingers. The basket is made by winding raffia on a reed base, in a laborious process in which an awl is used to insert the raffia.

left:
56 **Colombia,** Vaupes area of Amazon region. Tucano Indian. Basket tray, woven reed and vegetable fibers (diameter 58 cm). Baskets of this type are used to sift grain, and sometimes to pan for gold.

below:
57 **Rwanda.** Basket tray, vegetable fiber, dyed, coiled and wrapped (diameter 57 cm).
Lent by Agence de Coopération Culturelle et Technique, Paris.

opposite:
58 **Papua New Guinea,** New Britain. Buka tribe. Basket, natural-dyed vegetable fibers (diameter 87 cm).

59 **Rwanda.** Baskets with lids (height 15
to 23 cm). Baskets with this distinctive
peaked lid range in height from 15 to
250 cm. The large ones are used to
store grain.
*Lent by Agence de Coopération
Culturelle et Technique, Paris.*

Korea. Kae Jung Kwak. Gourd-shaped
baskets, handwoven rush
(25.5 x 16.5 cm).

Japan. A basketmaker weaves a
container in his workshop.

62 **United States,** Sea Island, South
Carolina. Basket, rushes, pine straw,
sweet grass, coiled and sewn with
palmetto leaf strands (height 33 cm).
Basketmaking is a traditional craft of
the black culture in the Sea Island
communities of South Carolina and
Georgia. The coiling and sewing
technique used here can be traced to
West Africa.

63 **Ghana.** Women master potters of the
Dowoda village near Accra fire
coil-built pots in a smoky open fire of
corn cobs, twigs, and palm stalks.

right:

64 **Senegal.** Water pot, hand-built clay (height 65 cm). African water pots frequently have rounded bottoms; they are carried on the head in padded rings and placed in shallow holes in the ground.
Lent by Agence de Coopération Culturelle et Technique, Paris.

below:

65 **Nigeria.** This craftsman uses a paddle to smooth the clay as he hand-builds a pot.

above:

66   **Spain,** La Galera, Tarragona. Rabbit's
maternity pot, wheel-thrown ceramic
(height 26 cm, diameter 46 cm). This
pot, typical of the La Galera region,
serves as a substitute for the rabbit's
natural burrow. The opening on top is
used to observe the mother and the
baby rabbits without disturbing them.

right:

67   **Spain,** Segorbe, Castellón. Snail
container, ceramic (height 36 cm,
diameter 25 cm). Snails are kept for a
month in this container and starved to
clean their intestines in preparation
for cooking.

opposite:

68   **Spain,** Aledo, Murcia. Spicery,
hand-built clay (height 20 cm).

69 **Spain,** Peruela, Zamora. Oven for baking bread, hand built of local clay (diameter 80 cm). Fire is introduced into the oven to heat it, then bread is baked in the heat retained.

70 **Spain,** Teruel. Pascual Laverías. Water
container for poultry, hand-built clay
(height 40 cm). Pascual Laverías is
the last potter of a village in Teruel
province, Calanda, which was once
famed for its hand-molded pottery.

71 **Papua New Guinea,** Sepik River District. Cooking pot, clay with zoomorphic decoration, hand-coiled and fired in an open fire (height 18 cm).

72 **United States,** New Mexico. Lucy Lewis, Acoma Pueblo. Jar, coil-built clay, slipped, painted, fired in an open pit (height 12 cm). The design of this piece is adapted from the distinctive pottery of the Anasazi people, ancestors of the contemporary Pueblo Indians. A revival of this craft has occurred in the Pueblo community during the past several decades.

73 **Peru.** Clay container in form of a llama
(length 29 cm).

74 **Mexico,** Patamban, Michoacan. Water
pot, ceramic (height 50 cm). This
traditional ''pineapple'' pot is produced
by men in the Patamban area.

78 **Nepal.** Chunar people. Container *(theki),* chiseled wood, brass (height 21 cm). Use of the theki is believed to date from the period when the Kathmandu Valley was settled by dairy farming peoples. Today they are still used by Nepalese farmers for making yogurt and storing dairy products such as butter and ghee.

79 **Ethiopia.** Footed food container with lid, carved wood (height 34 cm).

80 **Netherlands.** Maria van Kesteren.
Containers, bleached elmwood
(diameter: left 11 cm; right 25 cm).

81 **Sweden.** Sven Hägg. Bowl, lathe-turned
applewood (diameter 16 cm).

82 **Denmark.** Anni and Bent Knudsen.
Cocktail shaker, sterling silver
(height 29 cm).

above, right:

83 **Nepal.** Bhai Kazi Tamrakar. Water
container (*gagri*), hammered and
welded brass (height 37.5 cm). Vessels
of this type have been commonly used
to carry drinking water in Nepal since
the twelfth century. Full of water, they
are considered to be good omens,
and they are placed on both sides of
the path when one sets off on a journey.
An empty gagri seen at the time of
leaving home is a bad omen.

84 **India,** Gujarat. Water containers (*beda*), hammered copper (height of each about 25 cm). Two containers, stacked, form the piece at right.

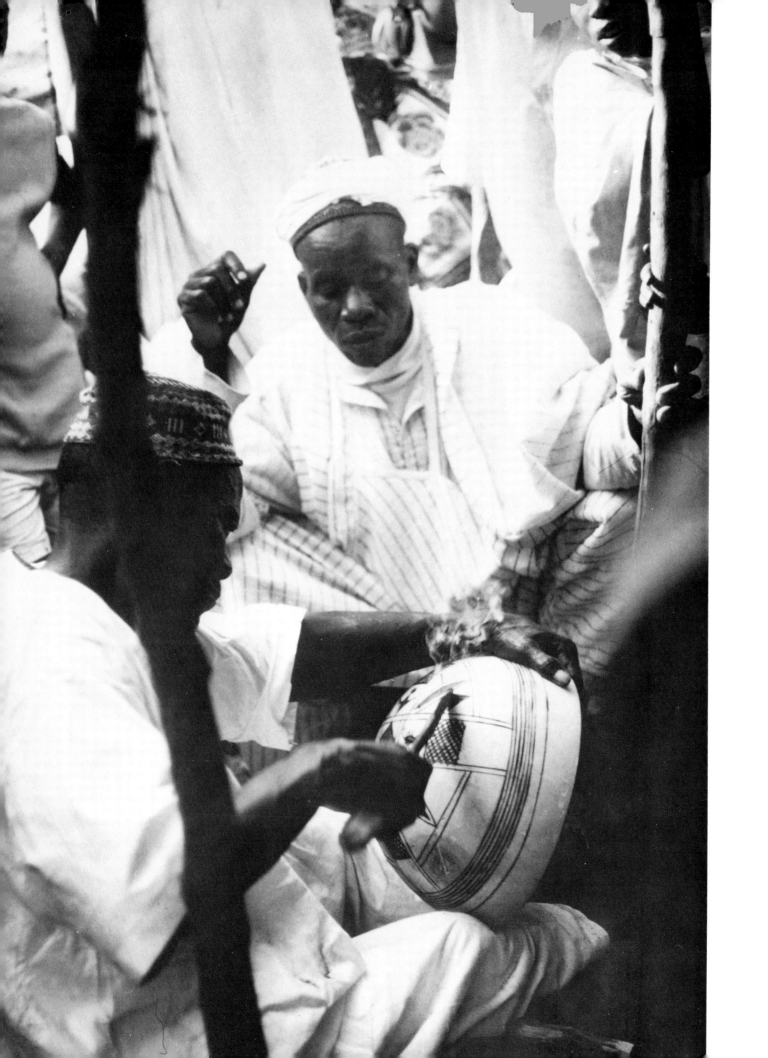

opposite:

85 **Nigeria.** Using a red hot metal tool, this craftsman incises a pattern on a bowl cut from a large gourd. This technique, pyrography, is commonly used in many parts of the world.

right:

86 **Mali and Niger.** Spoons, gourd, incised with pyrography (length 18 to 25 cm).

below:

87 **Niger.** Bowl, gourd, incised with pyrography (diameter 31 cm).
Lent by Agence de Coopération Culturelle et Technique, Paris.

88 **Sweden.** Ulrica Hydman-Vallien, Kosta Boda Glassworks. Goblets, glass, free blown, hot tooled, and painted (height 20 cm).

89 **Ethiopia.** Horn cups (height 8.5 and 7.5 cm). These cups are used for drinking *tella,* a beer made from barley, and *tej,* a wine made from honey and hops.

90 **Sweden.** Ann Wärff, Kosta Boda
Glassworks. *Lovely,* glass bowl, clear
glass with etched figures (height 20
cm, diameter 27.5 cm).

opposite:

91 **United States.** Erik Gronborg. Tea set, pot and four cups, porcelain with decals and lusters (height: teapot 28 cm; cups 18 cm).

92 **United Kingdom.** Michael Casson. Jug, stoneware with combed decoration, clear glaze over slip, reduction fired (height 31 cm).
Lent by The Royal Scottish Museum, Edinburgh.

93   **New Zealand.** Mirek Smisek. Bowl,
salt-glazed stoneware (diameter
52 cm).

94 **Australia.** Fred Smith. Salad bowl with
two spoons; bowl, western red cedar,
laminated construction (32.5 x 27 cm);
spoons, red pine.

opposite, above:

95 **Indonesia,** Central Java. Spoons,
carved cow's horn (length 28, 25.5 cm).
These spoons, with traditional dragon
decoration, are used to serve rice on
special occasions.

opposite, below:

96 **Lapland.** Spoons, carved caribou horn
(length 12, 15 cm).

above:

97 **Sweden.** Algot Nordström. Ladles and
rack, hand-carved birch and applewood
(length of ladles 12 to 29 cm).

Seating

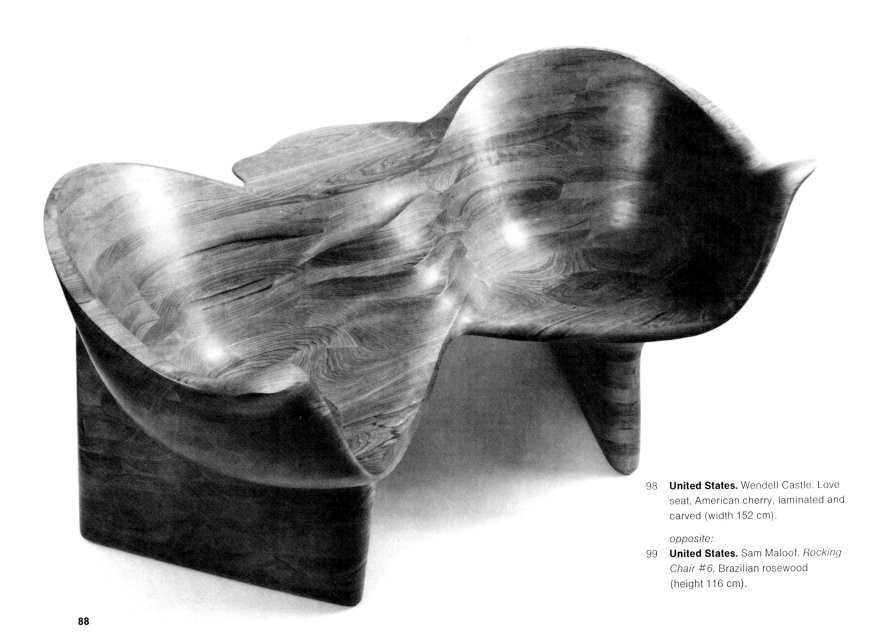

98 **United States.** Wendell Castle. Love seat, American cherry, laminated and carved (width 152 cm).

opposite:

99 **United States.** Sam Maloof. *Rocking Chair #6,* Brazilian rosewood (height 116 cm).

right:

100 **Ethiopia,** Walaga or Kefa province. *Jimā* stool, chiseled from one piece of wood (height 35 cm). Carved wooden stools are a common form of seating throughout Africa; in Ghana, for example, the ruler is said to be ''enstooled'' rather than ''enthroned.''

below:

101 **United States.** Jon Brooks. *Franklin Chair,* hand-carved black walnut, finished with Danish oil and wax (height 102 cm).

102 **Ireland.** John Surlis. Leitrim County chairs, ashwood (height: left 50 cm, right 85 cm). John Surlis is the last chairmaker to make chairs of this type, which are found only in Leitrim. The chairmaking tradition of the Surlis family, handed down from father to son, goes back six generations.

103 **Cameroon.** Bamileke tribe. Stools,
wood with beaded seats and bases
(height: left 38 cm, right 46 cm). The
Bamilekes traditionally use beads to
decorate works that are important as
ritual objects or as symbols of authority.
The crocodile, which forms the bases
of these stools, is a symbol of virility
and immortality.
Lent by Tribal Arts Gallery, New York.

104 **India,** Sankheda, Gujarat. Chair,
     lacquered wood (height 84 cm).

opposite:

105 **Togo.** Farmer's chair, carved wood (height 78 cm). This simple chair is easily assembled by fitting the seat into the back.
Lent by Agence de Coopération Culturelle et Technique, Paris.

left:

106 **Ethiopia,** western region. *Jimā* chair with back rest, chiseled from one piece of wood (height 100 cm).

107 **Dahomey,** Abomey region. Chief's seat, carved wood (height 51 cm).
Lent by Agence de Coopération Culturelle et Technique, Paris.

Coverings

108 **Australia,** Northern Territory. Aborigines from Oenpelli. Floor mat, dyed pandanus grasses (diameter 117 cm).

bottom:

109 **Bolivia.** Simona Borja, Indian from Argentine border region. Festive rug (*antemesa*), woven sheep's wool (length 214 cm, width 21 cm). Detail. Long, narrow rugs of this type are placed on the floor in front of the table on festive occasions.

preceding page:

110 **Sri Lanka,** Dumbara region. Mat, handwoven hemp (153 x 37 cm). Detail. These traditional mats, used both as carpets and wall hangings, are woven by men from hemp fiber found only in the Dumbara region.

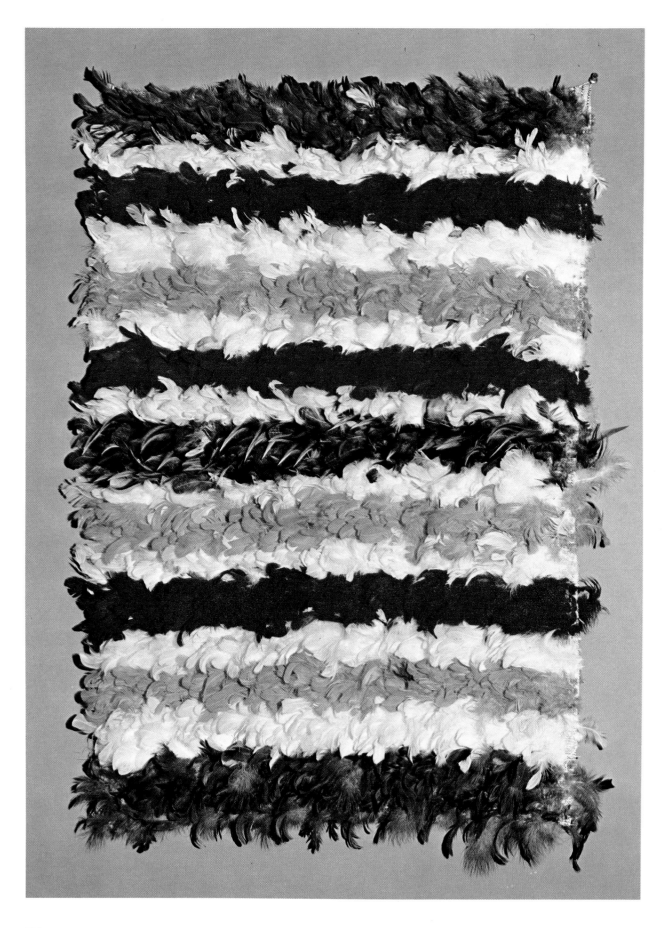

opposite:

114 **Spain.** Esperanza Rodriguez. Feather carpet (*alfombra*), woven cotton with natural and dyed feathers (90 x 42 cm). The technique, which is pre-Columbian, was introduced into Spain by the ''*Indianos,*'' Spaniards who returned to their native land after living in the Americas.

115 **Jordan.** Bedouins in Karak area. Ma'daba rug, handwoven sheep's wool (400 x 185 cm). Detail.

116 **Mali.** Blanket, handwoven wool strips, sewn together, natural dyes (250 x 140 cm). The six strips which make up blankets of this type are woven with traditional designs, carefully measured so that they will match when sewn together.
Lent by Agence de Coopération Culturelle et Technique, Paris.

opposite, above:

117 **India,** Madhubani District, North Bihar. Guna Omani. Quilted cover (*sujani*), layers of worn cloth quilted with cotton thread in geometric and figural motifs (110 x 180 cm). The images are symbols of fertility and prosperity: peacocks, turtles, fish, lotus flowers, elephants.

opposite, below:

118 **Ivory Coast,** Korhogo. Wall hanging, cotton cloth painted with mud dye (142 x 243 cm). Originally these cloths were used to make hunting clothes: the painted figures were thought to bring good fortune to the hunter. Strips of coarsely woven cloth are sewn together and painted twice with representations of witch doctors, masked dancers, and animals, usually in two or three rows. The figures are first drawn with a knife using a pale green vegetable dye; then the second dye, made from swamp sludge, is applied directly over the first, creating a fast black dye.
Lent by Agence de Coopération Culturelle et Technique, Paris.

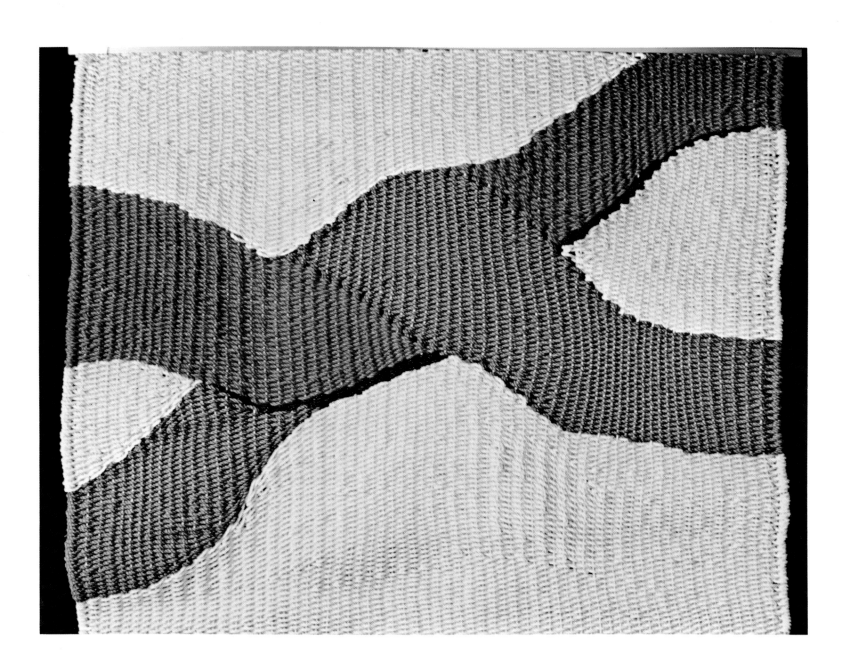

119 **Netherlands.** Wilhelmina Fruytier.
Acrobat, wall hanging, woven
polypropane cord (140 x 160 cm).

opposite:

120 **Canada.** Winnie Tatya, Eskimo. Wall
hanging, appliquéd wool (213 x 137
cm). The craftsman developed her skill
in sewing by making caribou skin
clothing for her family. Her images are
derived from Eskimo folklore and
Shamanist ''magic language.''

121 **Czechoslovakia.** Luba Krejčí. *Dreaming Dreamers,* hanging in frame, adaptation of traditional handsewn lace techniques (140 x 120 cm).

opposite:

122 **Hungary.** Irén Bódy. *Hussar,* wall picture, printed and dyed on cotton-linen (300 x 269 cm). The artist adapted traditional Hungarian techniques of printing and blue dyeing.

opposite, above:

123 **Nigeria,** Kano. Tie-dying. The dye pits
at Kano date back to medieval times,
when the town was an important
market center on the caravan
routes across the Sahara. Some
forty-eight of the pits, which measure
from four to twelve feet deep, are still
in use. To make the characteristic
patterns, commercially manufactured
white cloth is tied in small bunches;
over two-thousand ties were used to
make the pattern shown at right. Since
Kano is a Moslem community, the tying
is done by men, although wives may
help at home if needed. After the tying,
the cloth is soaked in a solution of gum
arabic and water, and then taken to the
dye pits. It is dipped in the rich indigo
dye and wrung out several times,
untied, and then hung to dry.

opposite, below:

124 **Nigeria,** Kano. Tie-dyed cloths are
draped on basket covers on top of the
dye pits to dry. At other times the covers
are propped up on long sticks and
used as sunshades by the workers.
After the cloth is dry, it may be
pounded with heavy wooden mallets to
achieve the glazed finish desired by
desert peoples because it sheds sand.

right:

125 **Nigeria,** Kano. Tie-dyed cloth hanging
(192 x 145 cm).
*Lent by Margaret M. Patch, World
Crafts Council, New York.*

Play

The pursuit of pleasure, the need to escape regularly from life's earnest tasks, is universal. Toys have calmed and delighted children, puzzles have intrigued their elders, songs have been sung, dances danced, and instruments played by all peoples in all lands. Backgammon pieces were found in the ruins of Babylon, dice-throwers are represented on Greek vases, chess has been played continuously for fourteen hundred years, lutes and harps almost three thousand years old have been taken from Egyptian tombs in good condition.

All manner of toys and games were known to the ancients. In early societies, as in the rural societies of our own time, periods of work and leisure (or rest from work) were set by the basic determinants of life, by the weather and by the seasons. In the enforced periods of leisure there was time to make the tools for work, and to make the tools—the games and toys and musical instruments—needed for contemplation and enjoyment.

Just as it has always been, many rural craftsmen of our own time make craft objects when weather or season prevents agricultural activity.

Homo ludens, man at play, is basic. His ingenuity in perfecting the tools of play often exceeds his gifts in the making of work tools, for all his joy, unconfined and untroubled, is lavished upon playthings. In no other creative form is invention so spontaneous or craftsmanship more loving. Delight in fashioning a toy is a natural extension of man's love for a child. The cheerful making of games anticipates the maker's pleasure in playing them. There is no greater witness to the affection that can be lavished upon an object than the master craftsman's attention to the *sound* of a musical instrument, made with painstaking attention to every element of its performance and its relationship to the hand of the performer. The making of objects of play remains a most gratifying human activity.

126 **Japan,** Shimane Prefecture. Tiger, papier-mâché (length 33 cm).

opposite:

127 **Japan.** In the middle of February children in the northern regions build snow houses called *kamakura* to honor the "God of Water" and hold parties in their igloos.

128 **Mexico,** San Martín Tilcajete, Oaxaca. Animal figures, carved wood (length 30 to 50 cm).

opposite:

129 **Thailand.** Dragon kite, rice paper, crêpe paper, bamboo, hand painted (length 914 cm).

130 **Spain,** Villafranca de los Caballeros, La Mancha. Cricket cage, clay (diameter 15 cm). Children place crickets in the cage to make a simple music box.

opposite, above:

131 **Switzerland.** Whistle, pyrographed wood (length 18 cm). This whistle in the form of a warbler simulates the warbler's sound when blown.

opposite, below:

132 **Austria.** Uli Mosel-Bauer. Baby's teething ring with rattle, sycamore wood, silver, violet root (overall length 15 cm). The *Veilchenwurzel* (violet) root has been used for centuries in Austria to quiet babies.

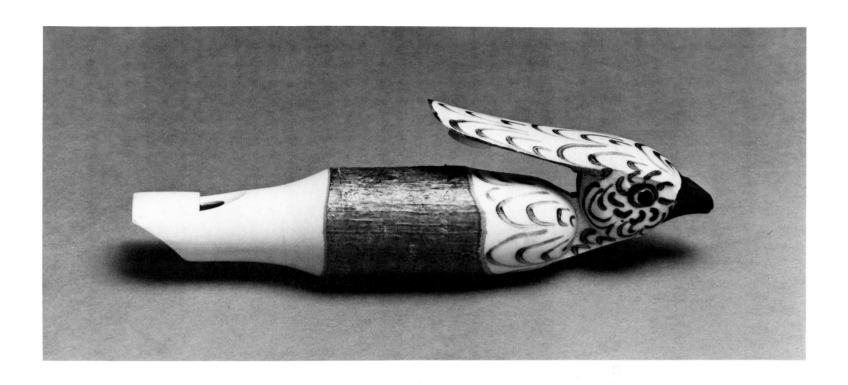

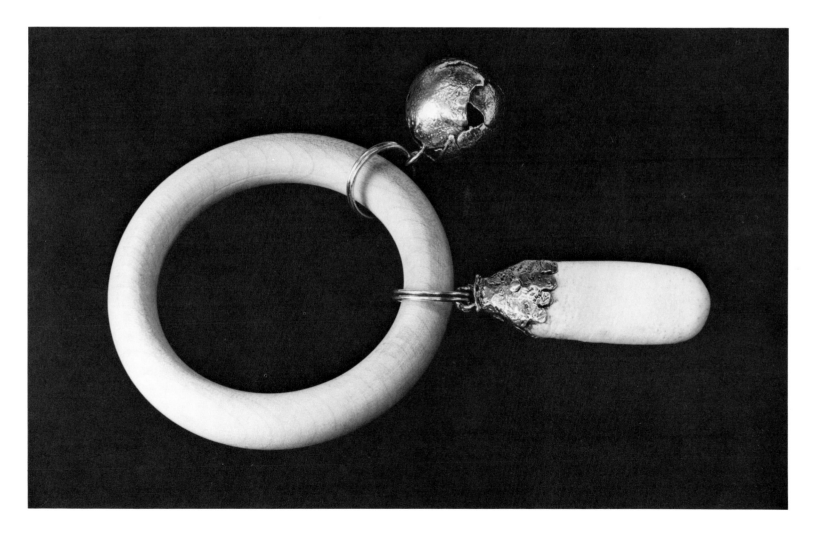

133 **United States,** New Mexico. Helen Cordero, Cochiti Pueblo Indian. Storyteller figure, hand-built of local clays, painted (height 26 cm). The mouth is open because the storyteller is chanting; the eyes are closed for thinking.

opposite:

134 **Mexico.** Candelario Medrano. *Noah's Ark,* molded clay sculpture (height 48 cm).

135 **Mexico.** Teodora Blanco. "Embroidered" doll, hand-built unglazed clay, applied clay decoration (height 51 cm).

opposite:

136 **United Kingdom.** Sam Smith. *Coupleboats,* carved and painted wood (length 31 to 37 cm). "Coupleboats have only two people on board—a man and a woman. When I first made them the pair were young and sort of beautiful. Wearing their wedding clothes, they went afloat on the Sea of Marriage with never a thought for the hazards ahead. In later versions—and some are here—the couple became more aware. When they embarked, they took their problems with them—uneasy companions they could not overlook. There is a certain amount of simple word-play in the titles: words, like people, have more in them than first meets the eye."
Above: Witherington. "A lazy lion-tamer is a poor mate even for a plain bride—especially when he brings his lioness along. The name 'Witherington' has no special significance except that it is rather hollow sounding."
Below, clockwise from upper left: A Man Punting Alone, Bull's-Eye, Custer, Joness of Pill, Witherington, A Dream Lasts Longer.
Lent by the Crafts Advisory Committee, London.

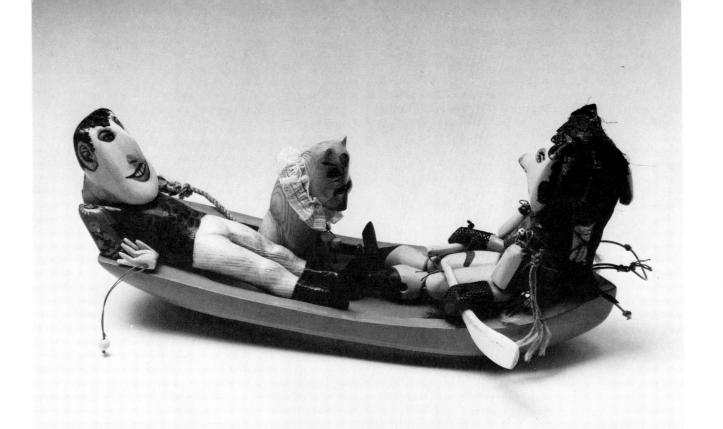

137 **United Kingdom.** Sam Smith. *Tmith,* carved and painted wood sculpture with sisal, rope, and velvet (height 75 cm, length 75 cm). The main figure is part woman, part lion; the small attendant figures are detachable and can be placed on the main figure in any order.

138 **Mexico,** Metepec, State of Mexico. *Pegasus,* molded clay figure (height 56 cm). The rearing horse is traditional in Metepec ceramics. The tail of the horse serves as a third support.

139 **Mexico,** Ameyaltepec, Guerrero.
Figures, hand-molded local clay
(height 15 cm).

opposite:

140 **Peru.** Carved wooden toys (length 30
cm). The figures move when the
hanging wooden blocks are pulled.
Left: men sawing wood; *right:* bull-
fighter and bull.

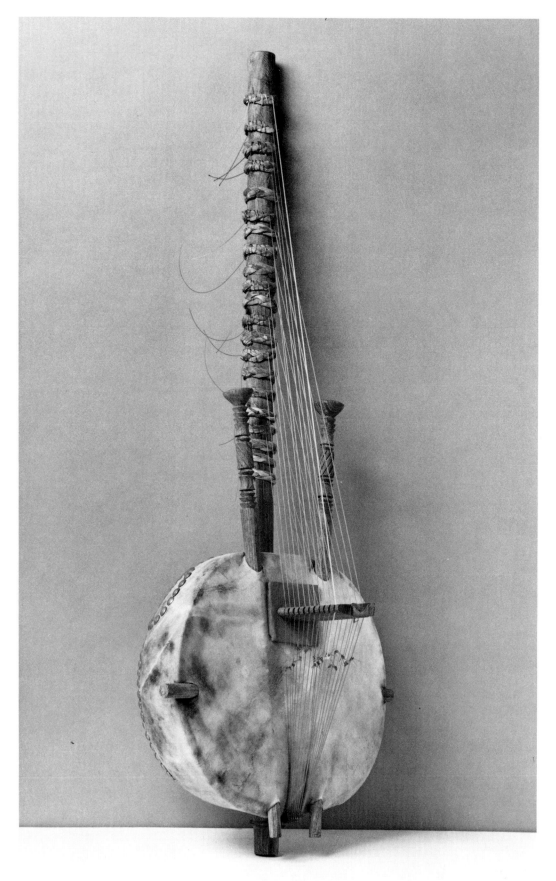

141 **Senegal.** *Kora,* twenty-one string musical instrument, gourd, hide, and wood (height 110 cm).
Lent by Agence de Coopération Culturelle et Technique, Paris.

opposite:

142 **Mali.** A Peul minstrel of the Timbuctoo region playing a four-string lute.

143 **Niger.** Hausa tribe. Double gong, forged metal (length 27.5 cm). Gongs of this type are used to announce the approach of a chief.
Lent by Agence de Coopération Culturelle et Technique, Paris.

opposite, below:

144 **Ethiopia.** *Masenko,* traditional stringed instrument with bow; carved wood and hide (length 82 cm).

145 **India,** Madras. *Ek-tara,* folk musical instrument, wood (height 23 cm, diameter 18 cm). This miniature well is both a percussion and a stringed instrument. When the bird is moved, the string running through the center of the well pulls a clapper on the bottom. The string can also be plucked. The ek-tara is used to accompany folk ballad singers in southern India.

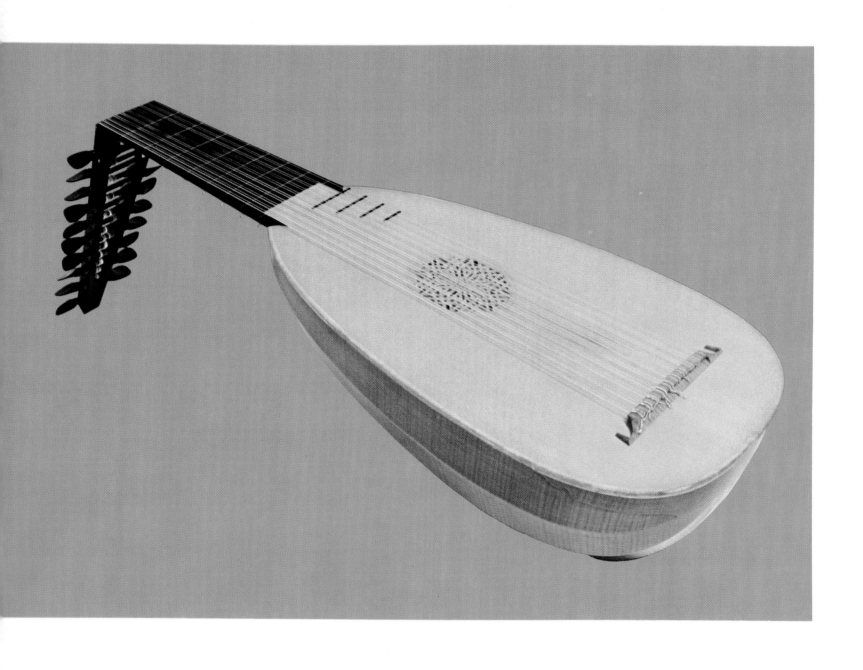

148 **Indonesia,** Western Java. *Angklung,*
musical instrument, bamboo (height
43 cm). This instrument is one of a set,
varied in size according to pitch which
together produce the pentatonic scale.
The set is used in harmony as an
orchestra on special occasions.

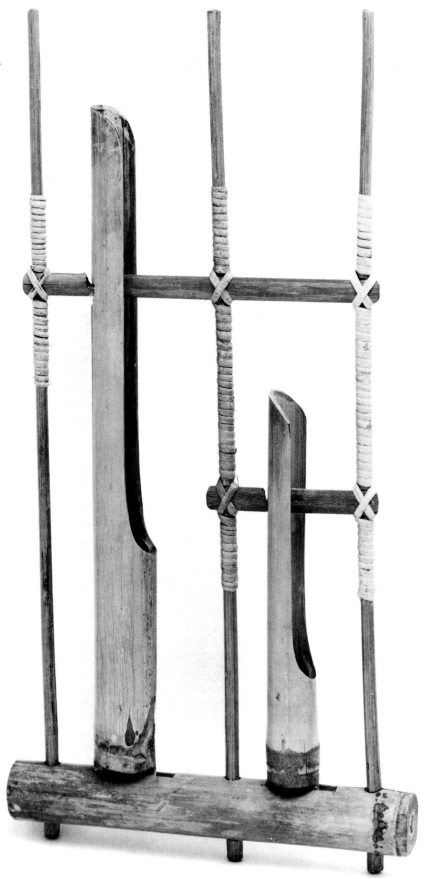

149 **Niger.** Hausa tribe. Tom-tom, wood and leather drum (height 48 cm).
Lent by Agence de Coopération Culturelle et Technique, Paris.

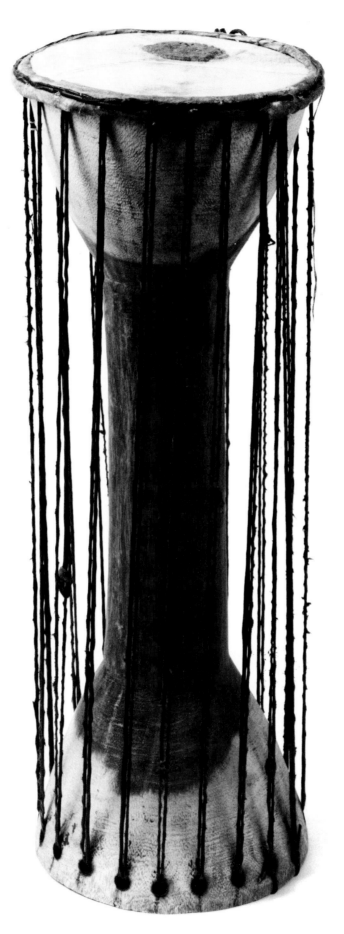

150 **Poland.** Push toy, painted wood with feathers (width 23 cm).

opposite:

151 **Switzerland.** Thomas Dubs. *Pegasus,* painted wood toy (24 x 26 cm). ''The little balls are pieces of sugar for Pegasus. He gets all three, nevertheless he is not kind and throws the whole family.''

152 **Japan.** Kokeshi dolls, lathe-turned
wood, painted (height of tallest 19 cm).
Each region of Japan produces its
distinctive Kokeshi doll, painted and
signed according to tradition. It is said
that the dolls evolved from the shape
of a pacifier.
*Lent by Göran Holmquist, World Crafts
Council, New York.*

opposite:

153 **Netherlands.** Lies Cosijn. Ceramic
chess set, white clay, blue and black
slip, opaque glaze (board: 100 x 100
cm; tallest piece 15 cm). Detail *below.*

154 **Indonesia,** West Java. Puppets, wood, carved and painted (height 66 cm). Detail. Puppets have been used in Indonesia for centuries to enact the moralistic Wayang plays. They are highly stylized in deference to Islamic prohibition of realistic images.

opposite:

155 **India,** Sankheda, Gujarat. Baby walker, lathe-turned wood, lacquered (height 57 cm). This toy is used to encourage a child learning to walk: as the walker is pushed, parrots on the sides rotate.

Ritual and Celebration

Pageantry and public performance lift hearts everywhere. No village, no city, no country, no tribe, no church, fails to celebrate signal events, joyous or solemn. There is a kinship of spirit in the festivals of the saints in Catholic countries, the Hindu Festival of the Lights, the tribal dances of Africa and Oceania, the Mexican Dance of Death, even in a marching parade marking a national holiday. Each is a witness to the *extraordinary* character of the event. Man celebrates occasionally, not regularly, and for special causes, religious, mystical or secular. The celebration, like a theatrical performance, requires careful design and preparation. As in the theater, there are actors, each with a part that must be studied and practiced to achieve a polished performance; and, as in the theater, there are settings and costumes to be made. Their uniqueness must reflect the singularity of the event, their brilliance must dazzle the beholder and accentuate the symbolic or illusionistic experience. In many religious, civic, and tribal festivals, the tradition of centuries dictates precisely the form and detail of the costumes worn. For the most part, celebrations *are* traditional and their enactment follows exact prescriptions. But in the painting of a mask, or the pattern of a robe, or the carving of a pole, intriguing variations of color and style are encountered. The craftsman's sense of invention and fantasy, far from being stifled by custom, is heightened by his own involvement in the event.

The craftsman's contribution to successful performance is integral, for it is he who provides the very materials without which the event becomes drab and ordinary. The making and using of costumes and masks, sceptres and wands, puppets and their stages, inanimate beasts and portable trees, castle and temple facades, and all of the other magic artifices of pageantry, enrich man's beliefs and whet his appetite for proclamation.

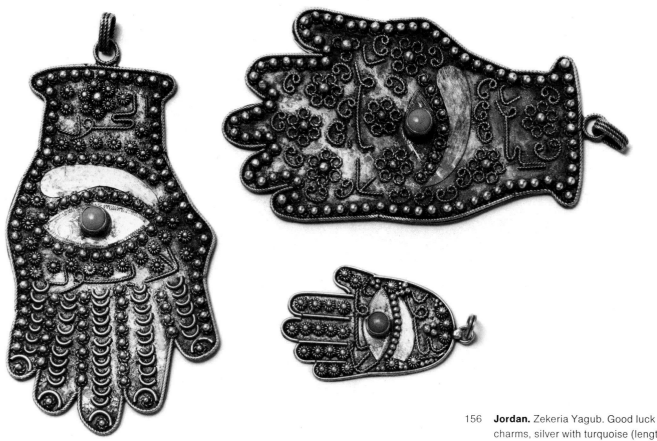

156 **Jordan.** Zekeria Yagub. Good luck charms, silver with turquoise (length of longest 12 cm). The Middle Eastern "lucky hand" traditionally offers protection against the evil eye.

preceding page:

157 **Switzerland.** Men of Appenzell Canton
create highly ornate bonnets to wear in
celebrations every December 31 and
January 13 (New Year's Eve of the
Julian calendar). The bonnets, made
of wood, wire, and cotton trimmed with
tinsel, trinkets, and beads, have
representations of Alpine scenes and
events in Swiss history. The attached
masks are made of wax.

opposite:

158 **India.** Haryana, Punjab. Embroidered hanging (*phulkari*), silk embroidery on handspun cotton cloth (140 x 220 cm). Embroidery has long been important in Punjab bridal costume and trousseau. According to tradition, upon the birth of a daughter the mother began work on an elaborate phulkari for the girl's wedding. Today, phulkaris depicting scenes from rural life and mythology are embroidered by women of the Jat community for presentation at weddings.

159 **United States,** South Dakota. Sophie New Holy, Sioux Indian. Breastplate, porcupine quills wrapped over rawhide strips, pendants of feather fluffs in tin cones, edged and lined with cotton fabric (length 47 cm). Porcupine quillwork is practiced exclusively by the Indians of North America. This piece is part of a dance costume used in tribal celebrations.

160 **Cyprus.** Christos Stavris. Decorative gourd, incised with knife (height 35.5 cm). Gourds of this sort are sometimes used to make wine bottles. This one is decorated with motifs of animals, flowers, and heroes of the Greek revolution.

opposite, above:

161 **Peru,** Cochas, Huancayo. Cipiriano. Gourd with burned and engraved design (diameter 35 cm). Decorated cut gourds are used as bowls and plates in this area.

opposite, below:
Detail of gourd, showing pattern of automobiles, people, and animals in city and country scenes.

162 **Ecuador,** Calderón, Pichincha. Cecilia Trujillo. Christmas crèche, figures of colored bread dough, lightly baked, varnished (height 10 to 18 cm). Traditionally, such bread dough figures were placed on the grave of the beloved on All Saints' Day, together with food and drink, so that the dead might share in the family feast. For the past twenty years the women of Calderón have made and sold the figures at other times of the year; these pieces are Christmas decorations.

opposite:

163 **Peru.** Hector Guzmán Urbano. *Retablo*, wood and paste altarpiece (height 89 cm). Such retablos are household shrines, their decoration combining folk and Christian traditions. The central section here represents the feast of the animals, the top contains a hat shop, and the bottom, a crèche. The paste used to form the figures, made of potatoes, gypsum powder, and honey or sugar, is molded by hand or in a press.

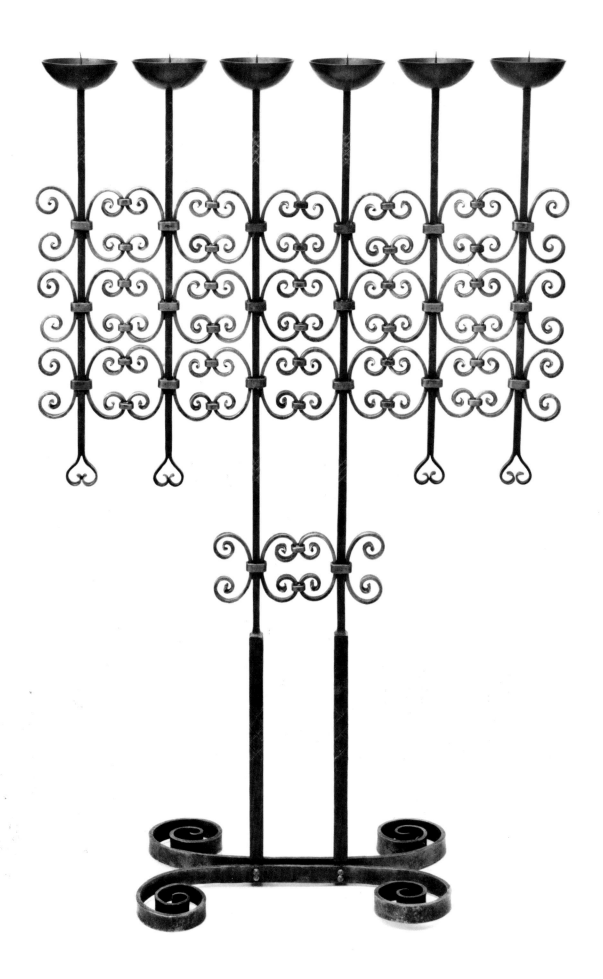

171 **Indonesia.** *Barong* mask, carved and painted wood (40 cm). The barong, a legendary animal, symbolizes the good, white-magic powers. The mask is employed in a dance to defend the community against evil, disease, and natural disasters.

opposite:

170 **Japan.** *Nebuta,* papier-maché floats representing men, animals, and birds, are lighted and pulled through the dark streets during the Nebuta festival in northeastern Japan. The festival is said to have originated from the legend of a resourceful warrior who tricked his enemies with Nebuta and scored a great victory.

opposite:

172 **Mexico.** Plumed headdress worn in Feather Dance in Oaxaca, celebration of the Holy Trinity.

173 **Cameroon.** Bamileke tribesmen wear beaded elephant masks in a ritual dance.

174 **New Hebrides,** Toman village, Mallicolo Island. Dance headdress, wood fibers and painted clay (height 73 cm).

opposite:

175 **India.** Kumbhakar potters. Ritual terra-cotta tiger, hand thrown and molded (length 34 cm). Animal figures of this type are made by the Kumbhakars, a community of potters, for the Bhils, a tribal people living in the forest areas of western India, who have used such figures as propitiatory offerings since ancient times.

following pages:

176 **Nigeria.** The face of the Alafin of Oyo, one of the four Yoruban tribal kings, is concealed from commoners by a veil of gold beads.

177 **Mexico,** San Martín Tilcajete, Oaxaca. Tiger mask, carved and painted wood (39 x 29 cm). Masks representing deities were of great importance in the religious rites of pre-Columbian Mexico, and their use survives in the secular ceremonies today. This decorative mask is similar to those worn in the Dance of the Tiger in Oaxaca. The ''tiger'' figure prevalent in Mexican folk art is actually a jaguar.

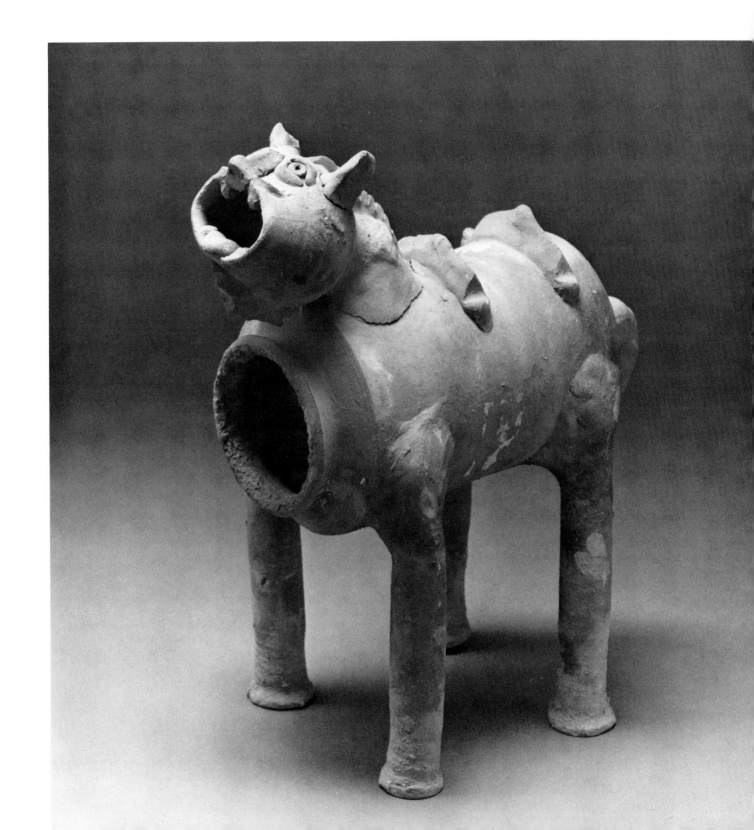

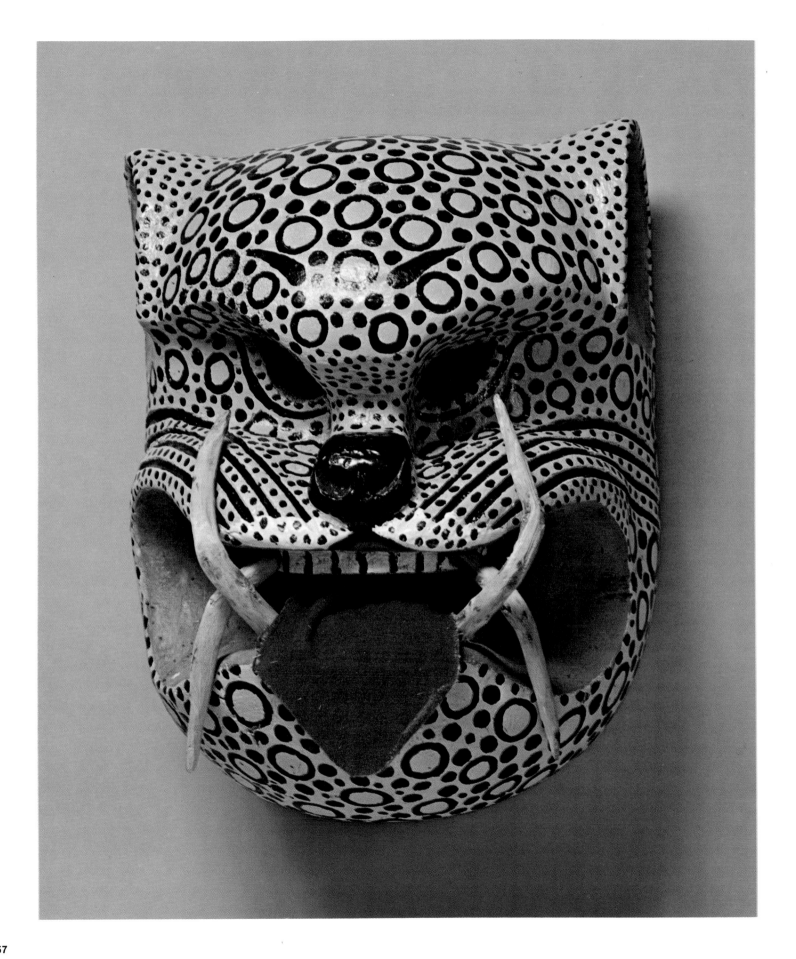

178　**India,** Ahmedabad, Gujarat. *Kalamkari* temple hanging, hand printed and painted, chemical dyes on cotton (190 x 380 cm). Detail of central panel depicting Mahisasura-mardini, one of the war-like manifestations of Durga, wife of Shiva, slaying the water buffalo demon. The outline of the design is printed by men; then the interior areas are filled in by women using a *kalam* (pen).

The Maker's Statement:

Clay

Although fiber was woven into cloth early in recorded history, pottery is surely the oldest and most universal craft. Clay, after all, is earth itself, found in one form or another on all the world continents, and used to make pots, vessels, plates and all kinds of containers in every age and society. In the hands of the early Chinese and Greeks, pottery became a high form of art, but it was also employed for utilitarian purposes, such as carrying oil and wine. In eighteenth-century Europe, decorated porcelains epitomized the effete elegance of court life. Early in the industrial age the mass production of pottery gave rise to abominations of taste, but reforms led in time to the sensitive design of machine-made ware.

Contemporary pottery runs the gamut from the simplest, functional pieces of the country potter to the extreme *tours de force* of the metropolitan designer-craftsman. Pots of classic beauty, made in traditional shapes and by traditional methods, are confronted by colorful, witty, and extravagant ceramic sculptures. Technical developments allow new exuberance in color and scale. Even the technology of the space age has been utilized: materials and processes developed to make the heat-resistant nose cones of spacecraft have been adapted to making harder, more durable pots.

179 **Australia.** Joan Grounds. Ceramic parcel, stoneware, iron oxide and low temperature enamels (9.5 x 40 x 26 cm). The parcel contains a dark stoneware thrown tea set.

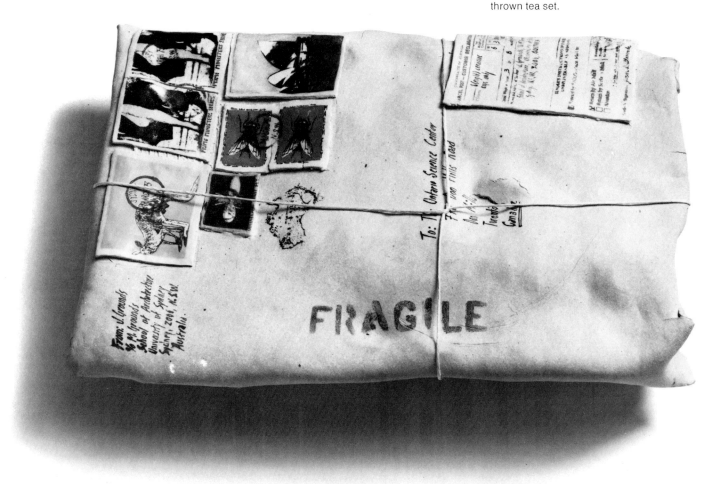

preceding page:

180 **United States.** Potter Toshiko Takaezu shapes clay on the wheel for one of her closed forms.

below:

181 **United States.** Jack Earl. *A duck can stir you all floating and pretty setting there making you think but as soon as you get to know him you find out he don't want nothing,* cast and modeled porcelain sculpture (length 130 cm). *Lent by Lee Nordness Gallery, New York.*

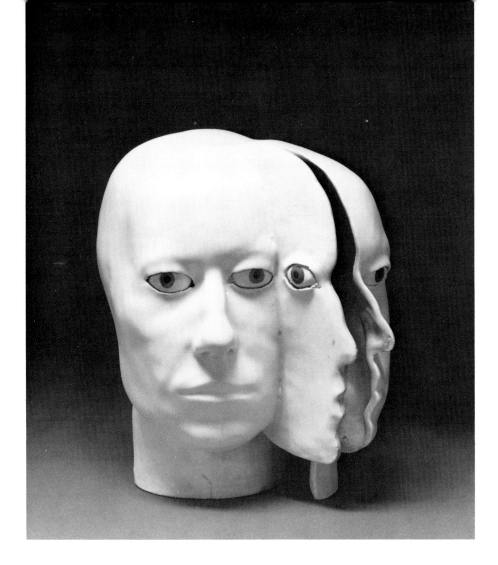

182 **Sweden.** Britt-Ingrid Persson. *Head,*
ceramic sculpture (height 25 cm).

below:
183 **United Kingdom.** Colin Pearson.
Porcelain pots, thrown and hand built
(height 14 cm and 25 cm).

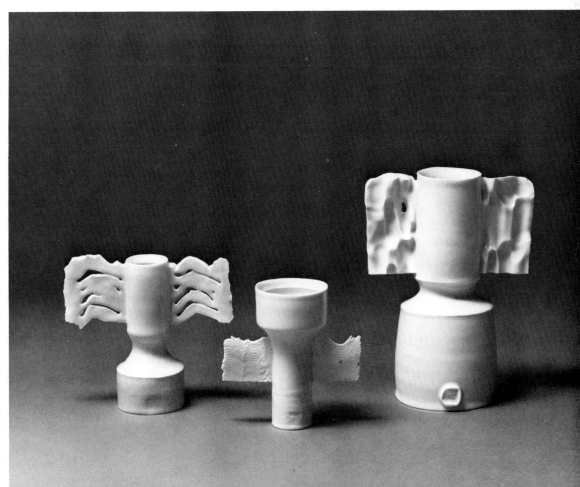

184 **United States.** Patti Warashina Bauer. *Customized Car Kiln,* hand-built clay with low fire glazes, underglazes, and china paint, wood and leather base (length 76 cm).

opposite:

185 **United States.** A gas-fired kiln, one of many types used by clay craftsmen today.

opposite, above:

186 **United Kingdom.** Jacqueline Poncelet.
Saucer and bowl, bone china, cast and
carved (diameter: saucer 15 cm, bowl
12 cm.)
*Lent by The Crafts Advisory Committee,
London.*

opposite, below:

187 **Canada.** Bailey Leslie. Deep compote
and footed pot, slab-built porcelain,
oxidation firing (height: compote 23 cm,
pot 41 cm).

188 **Japan.** Shôji Hamada. Ceramic platter,
Mashiko ware (diameter 57 cm).

189 **Venezuela.** Seka. Ceramic form, hand-built (height 27 cm, diameter 23 cm).

190 **Australia.** Marea Gazzard. *Delos II,* ceramic sculpture, hand-coiled and beaten, white high-fired matte glaze (64 x 72 cm).

191 **Finland.** Raija Tuumi. Stoneware pot,
thrown and perforated (height 29 cm,
diameter 59 cm).

192 **Canada.** Mary Keepax. Table, wheel-thrown white stoneware base with hand-formed porcelain flowers, glass top (height 35 cm).

opposite:
193 **United States.** Peter Voulkos shaping a large clay form.

right:

194 **Switzerland.** Ernst Hausermann.
Ceramic vase, slab-built stoneware with
ash glazes and printed decoration
(height 38 cm). The craftsman speaks
of an "alienation of the material
through the use of newspaper letters
and printing blocks. The images of the
ephemeral newspaper clippings on the
densely fired, unattackable stoneware
create tension."

below:

195 **Australia.** Peter Travis. *Musculloid,*
hand-built coiled ceramic sculpture,
high fired earthenware, slip and clay
glazes (54 x 66 x 18 cm).

opposite:

196 **Germany.** Ursula Scheid. Egg-shaped
vase, porcelain thrown in two parts and
mounted together, various glazes,
reduction fired (height 17 cm).

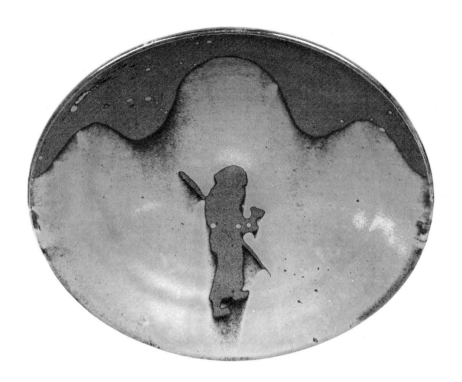

left:

197 **United Kingdom.** Bernard Leach. Stoneware dish, thrown, reduction fired, with tenmoku glaze (diameter 30 cm). This is one of a series of Pilgrim plates.

198 **France.** Yves Mohy. Stoneware vase, reduction fired (height 61 cm).

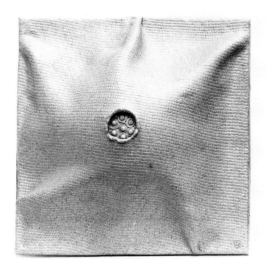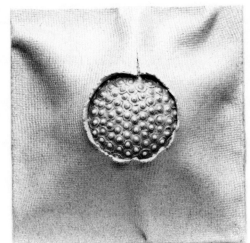

above:

199   **Netherlands.** Hans De Jong. *Three Tiles,* stoneware (each 30 x 30 cm).

200   **Switzerland.** Silvia Defraoui. *Ocre entr'ouvert,* sculpture, hand-built stoneware, palm ash glaze (67 x 45 x 24 cm). "As in the vegetal world, where closed forms become open, this piece shows the point of development when the inside and the outside come into equilibrium."

opposite:

201 **United States.** Wayne Higby. *White Canyon,* landscape container, earthenware, raku technique (height 30.5 cm).

left:

202 **Netherlands.** Kees Van Renssen. Ceramic sculpture (35 x 12 x 12 cm).

below:

203 **United States.** Paul Soldner. *Verushka,* ceramic platter, raku technique (49 x 60 cm).

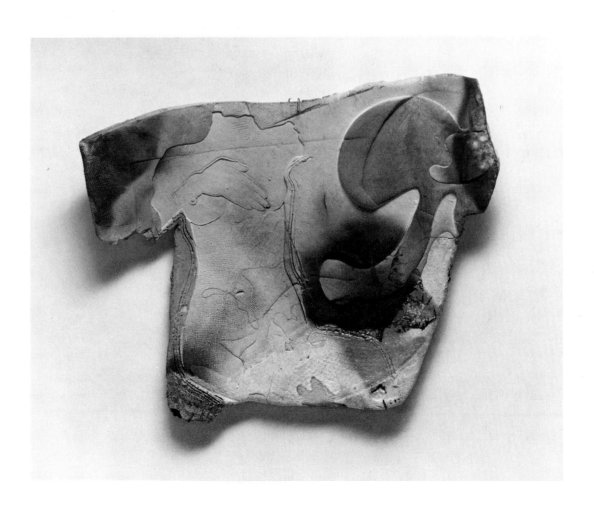

Glass

Glass is perhaps the craftsman's most versatile medium because of the infinite variety of shapes, colors, and textures attainable through the forming and firing of molten materials.

The medium has a long tradition. Molded glass of an opaque, ceramic-like quality was made in Egypt, possibly as early as 3500 B.C. Pre-Christian glass from Phoenicia is excavated frequently from the eastern Mediterranean littoral, and the Romans practiced glass blowing, using a hollow rod. In 1255, the first guild of glassmakers was formed in Venice, and glass has been continuously produced on Murano, the fabled Venetian island, since 1291. England in the sixteenth century, Germany and Bohemia in the seventeenth century, fostered the development of glassmaking enterprises which have survived without interruption over the centuries.

Leadership in twentieth-century glassmaking belonged successively to Austria and Germany in the 20s and 30s, to Scandinavia, notably Sweden, in the 40s, and to Italy in the 50s. The creation of handmade glass for domestic and decorative use remains vigorous on the European continent, while England and the United States have, in the present generation, produced glassmakers whose sense of invention and fantasy is fresh and stimulating. Glassmaking in Africa and Asia lacks a strong tradition and is limited. In North Africa and the Middle East, several traditional centers of glassmaking, such as Hebron, have been revived, and Mexico produces handmade table glass of "country quality."

Despite the constant search of innovative glassmakers for new forms and applications, no contemporary craft is more firmly wedded to the past, both as to technique and place of origin. The traditional, historic centers of glassmaking remain vital, and seem to disdain the passage of time.

opposite:
206 **Czechoslovakia.** Pavel Hlava assisted
by workshop of Miroslav Lenc.
Satellite, sculpture in two parts, garnet
glass, blown, cut, polished, and
punctured, using a new technique
developed by the craftsman
(35 x 45 cm).

207 **Czechoslovakia.** František Vízner.
Blue Form, Topaz Form, sculptures,
glass, cut, ground, sandblasted, acid
etched (diameter: blue 39 x 39 cm,
topaz 28.5 cm).
Czechoslovakia. Jaroslav Svoboda.
Glass Sculpture, cut, sandblasted, acid
etched (height 17 cm).

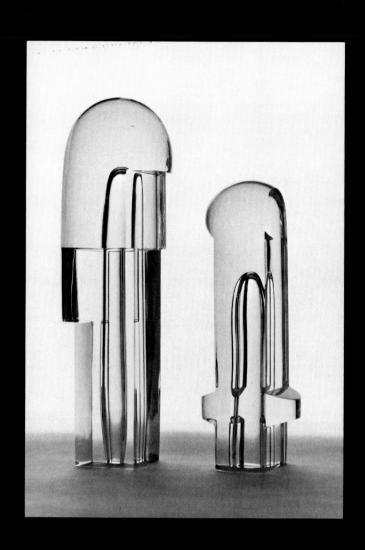

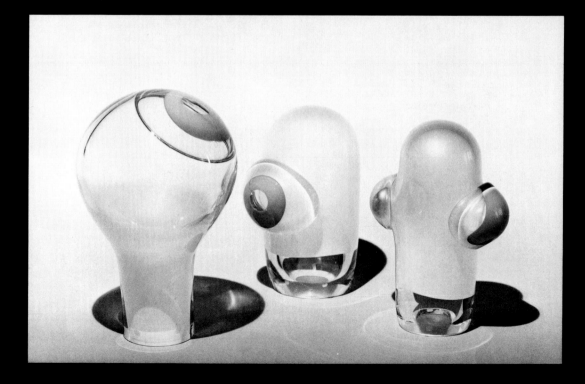

opposite, above:

208 **Austria.** Kurt Bloeb, with Lobmeyr Workshops. *Obelisks,* free-blown glass, cut, hand polished, with matte base (height: left 36 cm, right 28 cm). "I am a glass sculptor. I use the chisel for limited surface effect. . . . This time Egyptian mummies influenced the forms."

opposite, below:

209 **Netherlands.** Sybren Valkema. Sculptures, lead crystal glass with white opal and orange "eyes," white opalescent interior coating, free blown (height: left 30 cm, center 25 cm, right 26 cm).

below:

210 **United States.** Harvey Littleton. *Opportunity Trap,* sculpture, free-blown glass, ground and polished (length 56.5 cm).

211 **Sweden.** Bertil Vallien, Kosta Boda Glassworks. *Galax IX,* sculpture, lead crystal glass, cast and cut, wooden base (24 x 15 cm).

212 **Czechoslovakia.** Aleš Vašíček. *Fourth Dimension,* sculpture in four pieces, clear lead crystal glass, cut and polished to achieve plane surfaces (24 x 22 cm).

213 **United States.** Dick Marquis, assisted by Ro Purser and Terry Eaton. *Circus Teapot, Crazy-Quilt Teapot, Red and White Checkerboard Teapot,* non-functional teapots, blown glass, murrini technique, adaptation of seventeenth-century Italian cane techniques (height of tallest 19 cm).

214 **United States,** Joel Phillip Myers. *Bloomington Bloom III and IV,* sculptures, glass, silver nitrate, murrini technique, hot tooled, optik patterned (height: left 24 cm, right 29 cm).

Metal

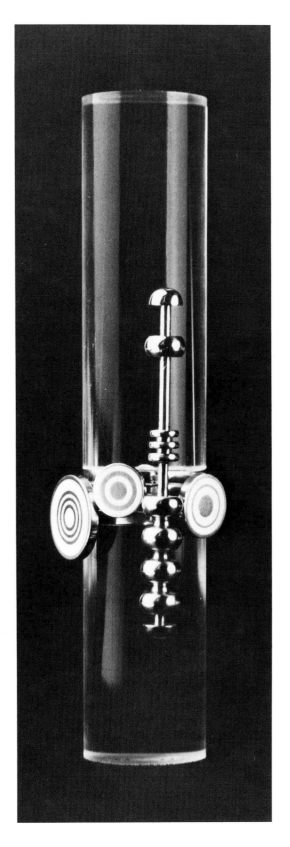

Man progressed from the Stone to the Bronze Age over five thousand years ago. It is believed that tools and weapons were fashioned of metal, and casting invented, before 3500 B.C. in the Middle East, and that copper and tin were brought from Central Europe for manufacture in Ancient Greece. The glorious bronze and iron artifacts of the Chou Dynasty, the classical age of China, were made in the millennium before the birth of Christ. Throughout European history, metalwork has been characterized by the highest order of craftsmanship: Benvenuto Cellini is mentioned with Holbein and Leonardo, Fabergé with Renoir. The goldsmiths and silversmiths of England have traditionally held high status. In this century, an explosion of creativity in Denmark and Mexico has given silversmiths a prominent role in their nations' cultural and economic growth.

The contemporary metalworker, for the most part, uses methods inherited from the past in the cutting and shaping of his materials, but contemporary *expression* in metal has been influenced profoundly by the movements of twentieth-century art. In Austria, Germany, Holland, Italy, Scandinavia, and the United States, the working of metal has strong architectural or sculptural overtones, and the forms of contemporary painting are frequently echoed.

The contemporary jeweler gives new exuberance to an ancient art form. Jewelry today has escaped from the confinement of miniaturism. Bold design, expansive forms, large scale and massive weight are exciting departures from tradition. New combinations of elements, the joining of metal with plastics and other synthetic materials, also make for vitality.

As in all other media, experimentation in one culture is matched by adherence to long tradition in another. Much of the metalwork of Africa, the Middle East and Asia is made today precisely as it was in the past.

216 **United Kingdom.** Wendy Ramshaw. Four rings with stand, gold, silver, enamel, perspex stand (diameter 2.5 cm).

opposite:
217 **United Kingdom.** Jeweler Wendy Ramshaw at her lathe.

218 **Germany.** Wolfgang Tümpel. Tea
container, fabricated from sterling
silver wires (height 14 cm).

above, right:

219 **United States.** Gary Noffke. Goblet,
18-carat gold seamless hollowware
with chased surface decoration
(height 16 cm).

220 **United Kingdom.** Michael Rowe.
Pomander, sterling silver with
removable units (height 22 cm).
*Lent by The Crafts Advisory Committee,
London.*

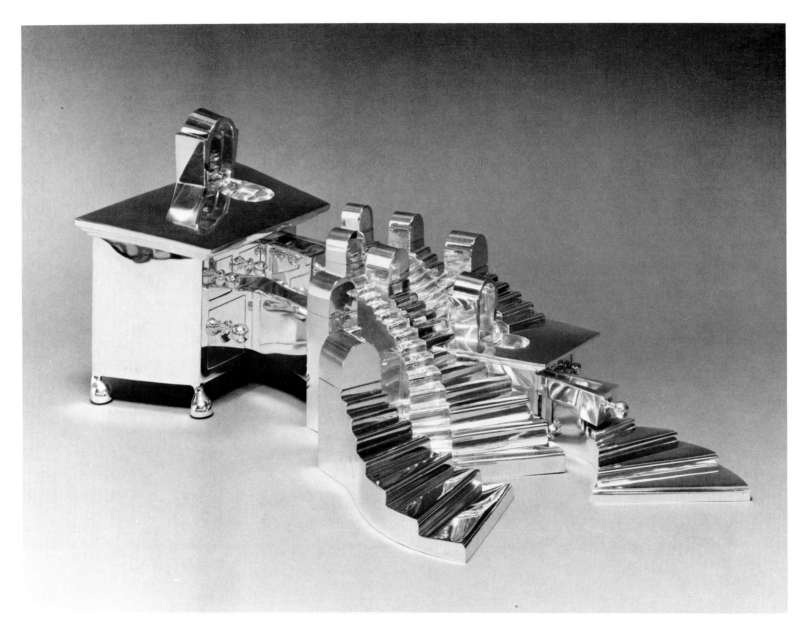

221 **Hungary.** József Engelsz. *Circus,*
metal relief, welded brass (diameter
67 cm).

opposite:
222 **United States,** Brent Kington.
Weathervane, mild steel and copper,
forged, embossed, and welded
(height 94 cm).

223 **United States.** Marci Zelmanoff. Neckpiece, fine and sterling silver with brass, fabricated from forged sterling wires and sheet; wrapped and twisted fine silver wire, assorted ornamentations (width 23 cm). "I want my work to have a sensual, organic fantasy, so that it can read both as adornment (in the magical rather than decorative sense) and as an object that can stand on its own apart from the body. I want it to reflect me — as a kid I always wanted to be a princess."

below, left:

224 **Switzerland.** Peter Fauser. Brooch, silver, gold, glass (diameter 8 cm).

below, right:

225 **Austria.** Josef Symon. Brooch, gold and silver plates, fabricated. (diameter 9 cm).

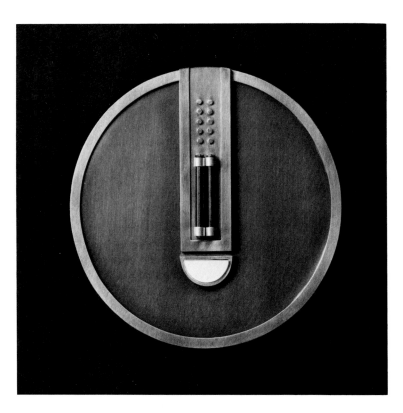

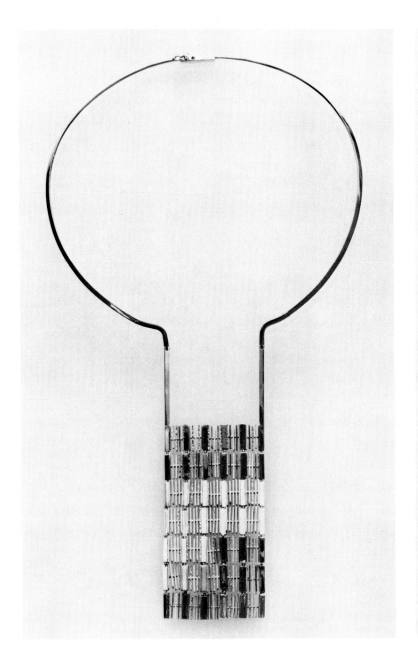

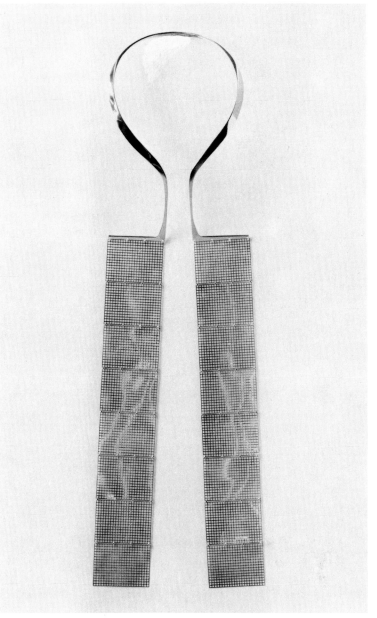

226 **Venezuela.** Harry Abend. Necklace,
white and yellow gold, fabricated
(pendant: length 8 cm).

above, right:

227 **Denmark.** Peter Vang. Necklace,
sterling silver, with rectangular screen
pendants (length 32.5 cm).

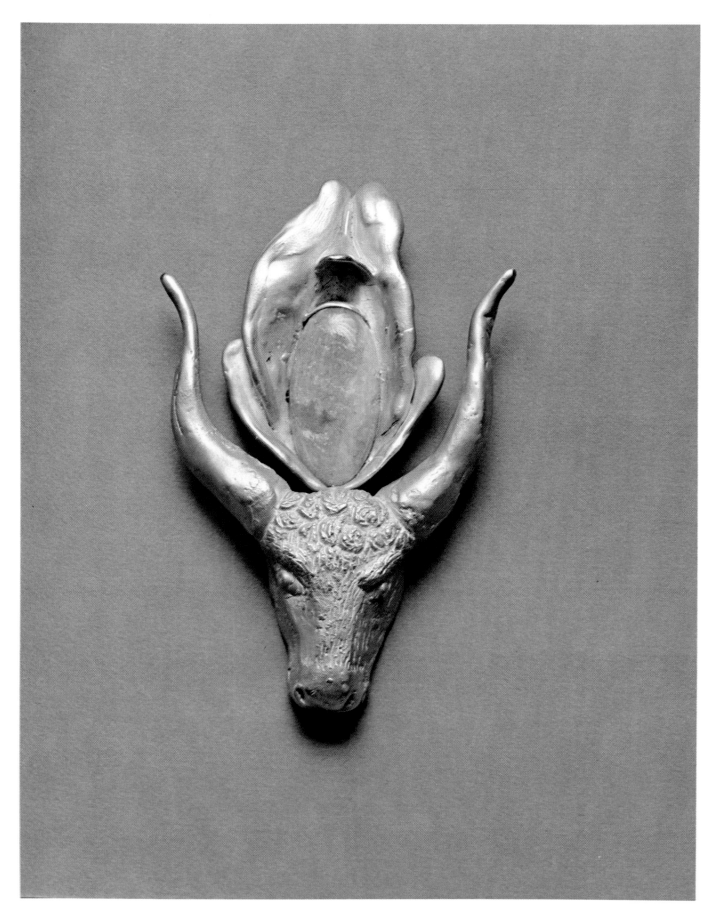

opposite:

228 **Switzerland.** Raffael Benazzi. Bull's
head brooch/pendant, gold and opal,
cast by lost wax method (height 10 cm).

229 **Finland.** Saara Hopea-Untracht.
Enameled dish, brush technique,
transparent colors on copper
(diameter 30 cm).

Fiber

Organic matter in the form of trees and bushes, plants, leaves, fronds, reeds and stalks, the coats of sheep and the larvae of moths and spiders, has been woven from the earliest times to provide shelter, clothing, and other essentials for comfort and use. The ancient Egyptians were superb weavers, producing garments of linen, baskets and tables of wicker, rush mats, and cord seats. Rope was woven extensively, and its use ranged from braids of false hair to ships' lines and rigging. The coastal plain of Peru has disgorged from the tombs of its ancient inhabitants a dazzling array of woven artifacts, miraculously preserved by constant aridity. For hundreds of years "silk from the Orient" was the image of luxury to Europeans; and Europe itself, from the Middle Ages onwards, produced weavings of lasting beauty and historical meaning. Virtually no region of the world is without a center for weaving. The names are magic, musical and nostalgic—Ashanti, Aubusson, Benares, Beauvais, Isfahan, Kashmir, Marrakech, Oaxaca, Paracas!

Craft, like art, is a continuum. The traditions of weaving have come down unbroken through the centuries, transposed drastically by the nineteenth-century power looms and twentieth-century computers of the textile industries, but remaining vital in the hands of contemporary weavers. Every conceivable variation is evident in handweaving today—the traditional basketmaking of a Philippine village coexists with the astonishing virtuoso creations of the off-loom artists whose works dominate the *Biennale* of Lausanne. Carpets are made by young girls in Tunisia or Iran as they have been for centuries, while fresh and wholly contemporary interpretations of woven form, using synthetic fibers, metallic thread, plastic tape, and other new materials, come from the ateliers of designer-craftsmen. Macramé and stitchery, presently in vogue, are traditional, but new applications and new styles lend vitality to old materials and techniques. Perhaps the most dramatic phenomenon in contemporary weaving is its wide variations of scale—from the exquisite small *molas* of the San Blas Indians to the gigantic wall hangings of the celebrated few.

230 **United States.** Ferne Jacobs. *Rainbow Basket,* knotted basket sculpture, fibers and moose hair (height 15 cm). *Lent by Fairtree Gallery, New York.*

opposite:

231 **United States.** Weaver Lenore Tawney knots the fringe of a wall hanging in her studio.

opposite:

232 **France.** Anne Terdjan. *Le Gros Arbre,* wall hanging, cotton cloth cut in strips (*lirette*) (120 x 124 cm).

233 **United States.** Lenore Davis. *The Garden of Eden,* sculpted pillow, cotton velveteen painted with dyes, trapunto quilting (78 x 65 cm). "This is a memento of a famous but fictitious place. It is an elegant and idealistic improvement over the cheap velvets and day-glow screen printing of the roadside souvenir stores."

234 **Switzerland.** Moik Schiele. *Black Sky,*
three-dimensional woven hanging
(180 x 116 x 105 cm).

opposite:

235 **Spain.** Marie Thérèse Codina. *Jouet
de l'air,* fiber sculpture, knotted sisal.
Detail (knot: diameter 40 cm).

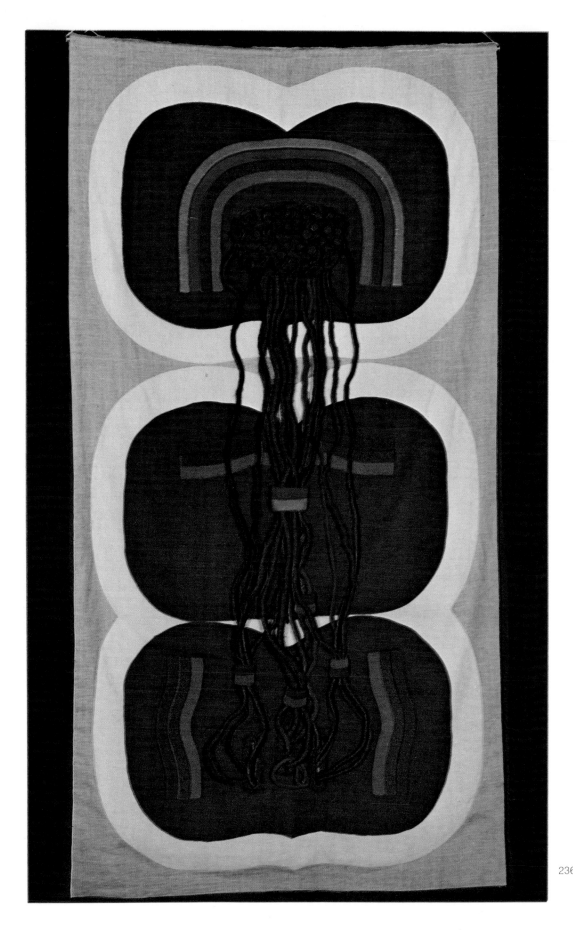

236 **Hungary.** Margit Szilvitzky. *Trilogy,*
wall hanging, linen and wool appliqué
on hemp (220 x 120 cm).

237 **Colombia.** Olga de Amaral. *Esculptura Simple,* wrapped and woven hanging, handspun wool and horsehair (307 x 198 cm). Detail, *right.*

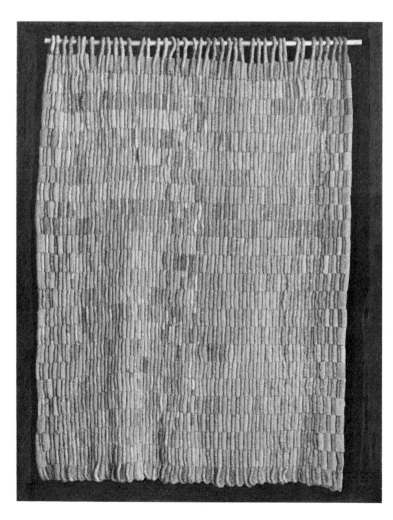

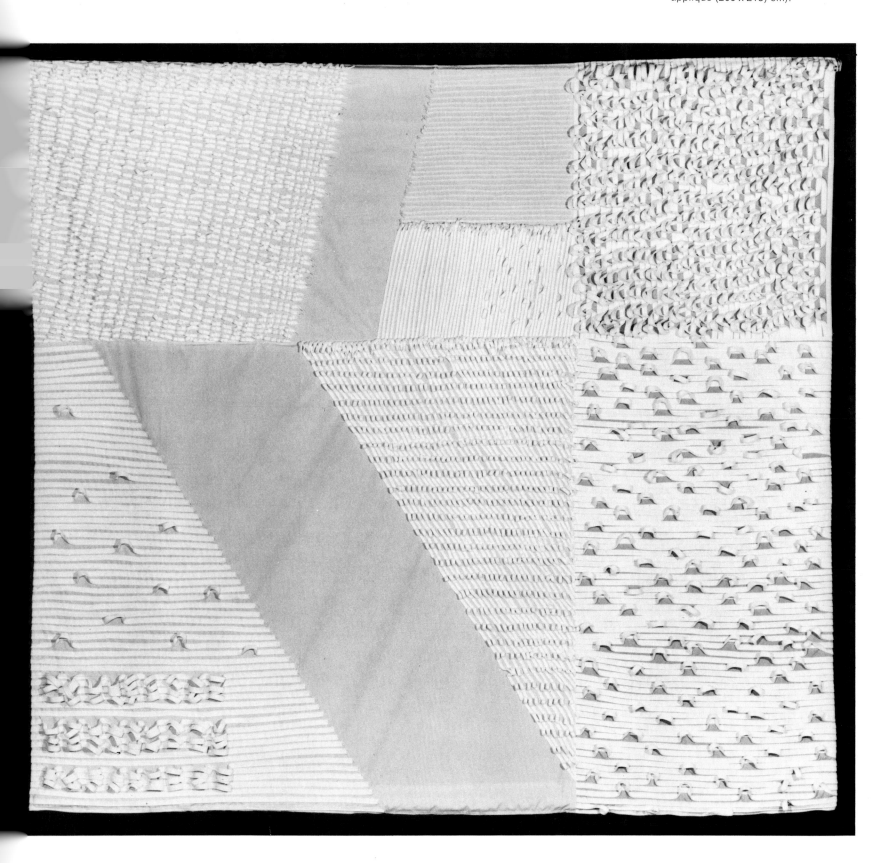

239 **Finland.** Kaarina Kellomaki.
International, silk-screen printing on
cotton. (1040 x 140 cm). Detail.

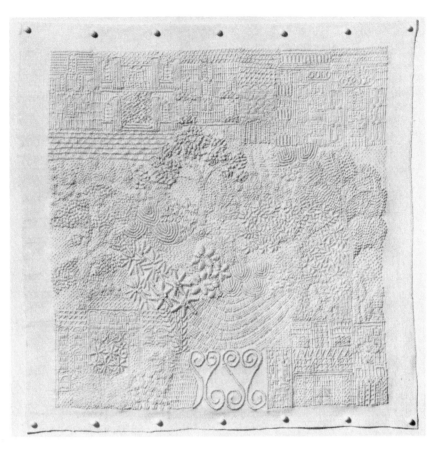

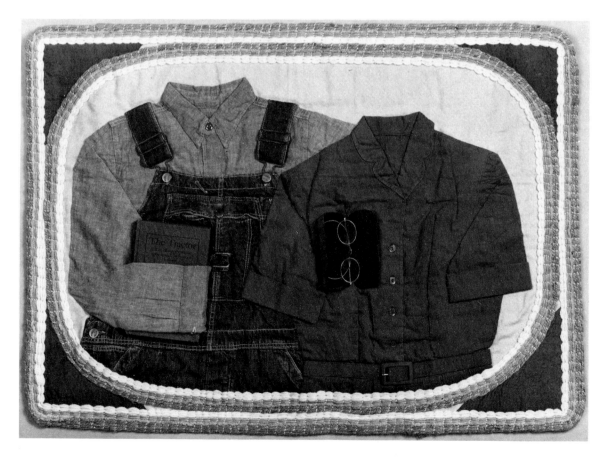

243 **Germany.** Peter and Ritzi Jacobi.
Structure, wall hanging, goat hair
(300 x 400 cm). Detail, *below.*

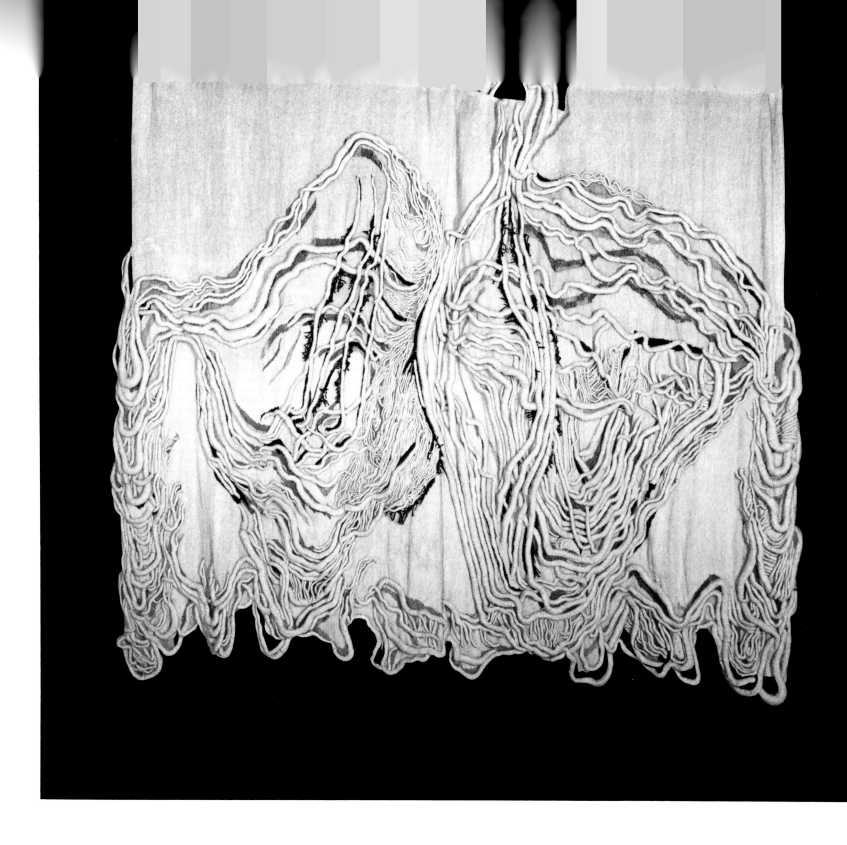

Selected Bibliography

by Peter H. Weinrich

GENERAL

Albers, Anni. *On designing.* Middletown, Conn., Wesleyan University, 1961. 82 pp, 12 ill.

Hansen, Hans Jurgen (ed). *Art and the seafarer: a historical survey of the arts and crafts of sailors and shipwrights.* London, Faber & Faber, 1968. 296 pp, many ill, biblio, index.

Jenkins, J. Geraint. *Traditional country craftsmen.* London, Routledge & Kegan Paul, 1965. xx, 236 pp, 185 ill. text figs, biblio, index.

Pye, David. *The nature and art of workmanship.* Cambridge, Cambridge University, 1968. xii, 101 pp, 31 ill, text figs, index.

Slivka, Rose (ed). *The crafts of the modern world.* With texts by Aileen O. Webb, Rose Slivka and Margaret Merwin Patch. New York, Horizon Press and World Crafts Council, 1968. 31 pp text, 404 ill, glossary.

GENERAL — Regional

Africa

Allison, Philip. *African stone sculpture.* London, Lund Humphries, 1968. viii, 71 pp, 99 ill, biblio, index.

Biebuyck, Daniel P. (ed). *Tradition and creativity in tribal art.* Berkeley, University of California Press, 1969. xx, 236 pp, 97 ill, biblio, index.

Fagg, William. *Tribes and forms in African art.* New York, Tudor, 1965. 123 pp, many ill, biblio, notes, list of tribes.

Fagg, William, and Plass, Margaret (eds). *The living arts of Nigeria.* London, Studio Vista Publishers, 1971. 160 pp, 175 ill.

Gardi, René. *African crafts and craftsmen.* New York, Reinhold Co., 1969. 243 pp, 192 ill, maps.

Leiris, Michael, and Delange, Jacqueline. *African art.* New York, Golden Press, 1968. xiv, 454 pp, glossary, biblio, index.

Sieber, Roy. *African textiles and decorative arts.* New York, Museum of Modern Art, 1972. 240 pp, 244 ill.

Trowell, Margaret. *African design.* London, Faber & Faber, 1960. 78 pp, 76 ill, index.

Wassing, René S. *African art: its background and traditions.* New York, Harry N. Abrams, 1968. xii, 285 pp, 264 ill, maps, biblio, index.

Asia

Adachi, Barbara. *The living treasures of Japan.* Introduction by Bernard Leach. Tokyo and New York, Kodansha International, Ltd., 1973. 67 pp, 96 color plates.

Bottrell, Fay (ed). *The artist craftsman in Australia: aspects of sensibility.* North Sydney, Jack Pollard, 1973. 160 pp, 269 ill.

Bühler, Alfred, Barrow, Terry, and Mountford, Charles P. *Oceania and Australia: the art of the South Seas.* London, Methuen, 1962. 250 pp, many ill, text figs, biblio, glossary, index.

Bussabarger, Robert F., and Robins, Betty Dashew. *The everyday art of India.* New York, Dover, 1968. xii, 205 pp, many ill, glossary, maps, list of dates, index.

Chattopadhyaya, Kamaladevi. *Indian handicrafts.* New Delhi, Allied Publishers, 1963. viii, 95 pp, 75 ill, biblio.

Force, Roland W., and Maryanne. *The Fuller collection of Pacific artifacts.* New York, Praeger, 1971. 360 pp, many ill.

Guiart, Jean. *The arts of the South Pacific.* London, Thames and Hudson, 1963. viii, 458 pp, 461 ill, glossary, biblio, maps.

Holme, Charles (ed). *Peasant art in Russia.* London, The Studio, 1912. xii, 52 pp, 550 ill.

Jenyns, R. Soame, and Watson, William. *Chinese art: the minor arts— gold, silver, bronze, cloisonné, Cantonese enamel, lacquer, furniture, wood.* New York, Universe, 1963. 461 pp, 221 ill, notes, index.

Jenyns, R. Soame. *Chinese art: the minor arts II—textiles, glass and painting on glass, carvings in ivory and rhinoceros horn, carvings in hardstones, snuff bottles, inkcakes and inkstones.* New York, Universe, 1965. 323 pp, 214 ill, notes.

Kim, Chewon and Won-Yong. *Treasures of Korean art: 2000 years of ceramics, sculpture and jeweled arts.* New York, Harry N. Abrams, 1966. xvi, 283 pp, 136 ill, glossary, biblio, chronology, maps, index. Published in the United Kingdom as "The arts of Korea."

Kojiro, Yuichiro. *Forms in Japan.* Honolulu, East-West Center, 1965. 184 pp, glossary, many ill.

Kühnel, Ernst. *The minor arts of Islam.* Ithaca, New York, Cornell University, 1971/London, George Bell and Sons, 1970. xii, 255 pp, 206 ill, appendices, biblio, index.

Lion-Goldschmidt, Daisy, and Moreau-Gobard, Jean-Claude. *Chinese art III: bronze, jade, sculpture, ceramics.* New York, Universe, 1961. 425 pp, 198 ill, chronology, biblio.

Mehta, Rustam J. *The handicrafts and industrial arts of India: a pictorial and descriptive survey of Indian craftsmanship.* Bombay, D. P. Taraporevala, 1960. xiv, 157 pp, 150 ill, glossary, biblio, index.

Mookerjee, Ajit. *Indian primitive art.* Calcutta, Oxford Book & Stationery, 1959. 79 pp, 49 ill.

Muraoka, Kageo and Okamura, Kichiemon. *Folk arts and crafts of Japan.* New York, Weatherhill, n.d. 179 pp, 160 ill.

Ogawa, Masataka. *The enduring crafts of Japan: 33 living national treasures.* New York, Walker/Weatherhill, 1968. xxi, 229 pp, many ill.

Oka, Hideyuki. *How to wrap five eggs: Japanese design in traditional packaging.* New York, Harper & Row, 1967. 203 pp, 222 ill.

Pope, Arthur Upham, and Ackerman, Phyllis (eds). *A survey of Persian art from prehistoric times to the present.* London, Oxford University, 1938-39: revised with addenda and corrigenda, 1964-65. 13 volumes: vols I-IV text, of which vol IV ceramics, calligraphy, epigraphy; vol V art of the book, textiles; vol VI carpets, metalwork, minor arts and index; vols VII-XII plates, of which X, XI and XII cover above texts; vol XIII addenda.

Richie, Donald. *Design and craftsmanship of Japan: stone, metal, fibers and fabrics, bamboo;* with *Katachi: Japanese pattern and design in wood, paper and clay.* New York, Harry N. Abrams, 1964. 2 vols, xxviii, 182 ill; xxiv, 170 ill.

Rowland, Benjamin. *Art in Afghanistan: objects from the Kabul Museum.* London, Allen Lane The Penguin Press, 1971. xiv, 93 pp. 214 ill, biblio, notes.

Wulff, Hans E. *The traditional crafts of Persia: their development, technology and influence on Eastern and Western civilization.* Cambridge, Massachusetts Institute of Technology, 1966. xxiv, 403 pp, 423 ill, biblio, glossary, index.

Yanagi, Sōetsu. *The unknown craftsman: a Japanese insight into beauty.* Adapted by Bernard Leach. Tokyo, New York, Kodansha International, 1972. 230 pp, 86 ill, index.

Europe

Aslanapa, Oktay. *Turkish art and architecture.* London, Faber and Faber, 1971. 422 pp, 282 ill, glossary, tables, biblio, maps, index.

Aslin, Elizabeth. *The aesthetic movement, prelude to art nouveau.* London, Elek, 1969. 192 pp, 123 ill, text figs, notes, biblio, index.

Bischofberger, Bruno (Sammlung). *Volkskunst aus Appenzell und dem toggenburg.* Zurich, Edition B-Press, 1973. 454 pp, many ill, biblio.

De Castro Pires de Lima, Fernando (ed). *A arte popular en Portugal.* 3 volumes. Lisbon, Editorial Verbo. 410 pp, 422 pp, 426 pp, many ill.

Delahaye, Gilbert. *Nouveau guide des artisans et créateurs de France.* Paris, Editions Robert Laffont, 1970. 239 pp, many ill.

Fél, Edit, Hofer, Tamás, and K.-Csilléry, Klára. *Hungarian peasant art.* Budapest, Corvina, 1958. 84 pp, 241 ill.

Hansen, H. J. (ed). *European folk art in Europe and the Americas.* New York, McGraw-Hill, 1968. 288 pp, 459 ill, text figs, biblio, index.

Holme, Charles (ed). *Peasant art in Sweden, Lapland and Iceland.* London, The Studio, 1910. viii, 48 pp, many ill.

Itten, Johannes. *Design and form: the basic course at the Bauhaus.* New York, Reinhold Co., 1964. 190 pp, 197 ill, index.

Jackowski, Aleksander, and Jarnuszkiewicz, Jadwiga. *Polnische volkskunst.* Vienna, Anton Schroll, 1968. 479 pp, 521 ill, biblio, map. Translated into English, 1969.

Matteini, Cesare (ed). *Handicrafts in Italy (Artigianato artistico italiano).* Florence, Ente Autonomo Mostra Marcato Nazionale dell' Artigianato, 1968. English, German and Italian versions in one volume. 559 pp, many ill.

Morris, William. *Architecture, industry and wealth: collected papers.* London, Longmans, Green, 1902. viii, 269 pp.

Naylor, Gillian. *The arts and crafts movement: a study of its sources, ideals and influence on design theory.* London, Studio Vista, 1971. 208 pp, 101 ill, biblio, sources, notes, index.

Oprescu, George. *Peasant art in Roumania.* London, The Studio, 1929. xviii, 182 pp, many ill, biblio.

Save, Colette. *Les artisans de France* (vol. 1). Paris, l'Estampille—Robert Morel, 1972. 303 pp, many ill.

Scheidig, Walther. *Crafts of the Weimar Bauhaus 1919-1924: an early experiment in industrial design.* London, Studio Vista, 1967. 150 pp, 92 ill, biblio, index of names.

Stewart, Janice S. *The folk arts of Norway.* Madison, University of Wisconsin, 1953. xviii, 246 pp, 157 ill, biblio, index.

Toschi, Paolo. *Arte popolare italiana.* Rome, Carlo Bestetti, 1960. 451 pp, 553 ill, biblio, English summary inserted.

Valonen, Niilo. *Treasures of Finnish folk art.* New York, Praeger, 1969. 230 pp, 210 ill, notes to plates.

Wingler, Hans. *The Bauhaus.* Cambridge, Mass., and London, The MIT Press, 1969. 653 pp, many ill.

The Americas

American Crafts Council. Specialized bibliographies available in clay (16 pp), enamel (4 pp), glass (8 pp), wood (14 pp). New York, American Crafts Council, 1973.

American Crafts Council. *Research in the crafts:* papers delivered at the fourth national conference of the American Crafts Council, 26-29 August 1961 . . . New York, American Crafts Council, 1961. 152 pp.

Christensen, Erwin O. *The index of American design.* New York and Washington, Macmillan and National Gallery of Art, 1950. xviii, 229 pp, 378 ill, list of illustrations, subject list, biblio, index.

Clark, Robert Judson (ed). The arts and crafts movement in America 1876-1916. Princeton, N.J., Princeton University Press, 1972. 190 pp, 295 ill, biblio.

Dockstader, Frederick J. *Indian art in America: the arts and crafts of the North American Indian.* Greenwich, Conn., New York Graphic Society, 1966 (3rd edition). 224 pp, 248 ill, biblio.

Dockstader, Frederick J. *Indian art in Middle America.* Greenwich, Conn., New York Graphic Society, 1964. 221 pp, 248 ill, maps, notes, biblio.

Dockstader, Frederick J. *Indian art in South America: pre-Columbian and contemporary arts and crafts.* Greenwich, Conn., New York Graphic Society, 1967. 222 pp, 250 ill, maps, biblio.

Eaton, Allen H. *Handicrafts of New England.* New York, Harper and Brothers Publishers, 1949. 374 pp, ill, index.

Eaton, Allen H. *Handicrafts of the Southern Highlands: with an account of the rural handicraft movement in the United States.* New York, Russell Sage Foundation, 1937. 370 pp, 114 ill, biblio, appendices on dyeing and colours, index.

Fondo Editorial de las Plástica Mexicana. *The ephemeral and the eternal of Mexican folk art (Arte popular Mexicano).* 2 volumes. Mexico City, Banco Nacional de Comerció Exterior, S.A. Spanish and English editions. 1971. 756 pp, many color plates and illustrations, biblio.

Harvey, Marian. *Crafts of Mexico.* New York, Macmillan Publishing Co., 1973. 247 pp, ill.

Hawthorn, Audrey. *Art of the Kwakiutl Indians and other northwest tribes.* Vancouver, Canada, University of British Columbia, 1967. xxx, 410 pp, 569 ill, appendices, glossary, biblio, index.

Kouwenhoven, John A. *Made in America.* New York, Doubleday and Company, Inc., 1948 (now in paperback). 303 pp, 16 ill, biblio, index.

Lichten, Frances. *The arts of rural Pennsylvania.* London and New York, Charles Scribner and Sons, 1946. xiv, 276 pp, many ill, index.

Nordness, Lee. *Objects: USA.* New York, Viking Press, 1970. 360 pp, many ill, index.

Osborne, Lilly de Jongh. *Indian crafts of Guatemala and El Salvador.* Norman, University of Oklahoma, 1965. xxvi, 278 pp, 82 ill, maps, appendices, biblio, index.

Wigginton, Eliot (ed). *The Foxfire book* (volumes I and II). Garden City, N.J., Doubleday (Anchor Books), 1971. vol I: 384 pp, 294 ill, index of people; vol II: 410 pp, 387 ill, index of people.

MEDIA

Clay

Berensohn, Paulus. *Finding one's way with clay: pinched pottery and the color of clay.* New York, Simon & Schuster, 1972. 159 pp, ill.

Brears, Peter C.D. *The English country pottery: its history and techniques.* Newton Abbott, David & Charles, 1971. 266 pp, 46 ill, text figs, notes, gazeteer, appendices, biblio, index.

Cardew, Michael. *Pioneer pottery.* London, Longmans, 1969. xvi, 327 pp, 57 ill, text figs, appendices, biblio, glossary, index.

Dickerson, John. *Raku handbook, a practical approach to the ceramic art.* New York, Van Nostrand Reinhold Co., 1972. 112 pp, ill.

Fagg, William, and Picton, John. *The potter's art in Africa.* London, British Museum, 1970. 48 pp, 32 ill.

Green, David. *Pottery: materials and techniques.* London, Faber & Faber, 1967. 148 pp, 42 ill, text figs, glossary, biblio.

Griffing, Robert P., Jr. *The art of the Korean potter.* New York, Asia Society, 1968. 131 pp, 106 ill, map, biblio.

Jenyns, Soame. *Japanese pottery.* London, Faber & Faber, 1971. xiv, 380 pp, 120 ill, appendices, biblio, map.

Leach, Bernard. *A potter's book.* London, Faber & Faber, 1940. xvii, 293 pp, 81 ill, text figs, index.

Leach, Bernard. *A potter in Japan 1952-1954.* London, Faber & Faber, 1960. 246 pp, ill, glossary, index.

Leach, Bernard. *A potter's portfolio: a selection of fine pots.* London, Lund Humphries, 1951. 16 pp, 60 ill, 14 pp.

Llorens Artiga, J., and Corredor-Matheos, J. *Spanish folk ceramics.* Barcelona, Editorial Blume, 1973. 240 pp, many ill. Spanish and English side-by-side in one edition.

Matson, Frederick R. *Ceramics and man.* Chicago, Aldine Publishing Co., 1965. 301 pp, ill, index.

Mikami, Tsugio. *The art of Japanese ceramics.* New York, Weatherhill/Heibonsha, 1972. 118 pp, 199 ill.

Nelson, Glenn C. *Ceramics: a potter's handbook.* New York, Holt, Rinehart and Winston, Inc., 1971. 348 pp, 526 ill, ref. tables, glaze and stain recipes, clay bodies, sources of material and equipment, biblio.

Okuda, Seiichi, Koyama, Fujio, and Hayashiya, Seizo. *Japanese ceramics.* Tokyo, Tōto Bunka, c1956. 35 pp English text, 187 pp Japanese text, ill.

Rackham, Bernard, and Read, Herbert. *English pottery: its development from early times to the end of the eighteenth century: with an appendix on the Wrotham potters by Dr. J.W.L. Glaisher.* London, Ernest Benn, 1924. xxiv, 143 pp, 207 ill, biblio, index.

Rhodes, Daniel. *Clay and glazes for the potter.* Philadelphia, Chilton, 1957. xvi, 219 pp, 25 ill, index.

Rhodes, Daniel. *Kilns: design, construction and operation.* Philadelphia, Chilton, 1968. x, 241 pp, 203 ill, biblio, index.

Rhodes, Daniel. *Stoneware and porcelain: the art of high-fired pottery.* Philadelphia, Chilton, 1959. x, 217 pp, 82 ill, index.

Rhodes, Daniel. *Tamba pottery: the timeless art of a Japanese village.* Tokyo, New York, Kodansha International, 1970. 180 pp, 151 ill, text figs, biblio.

Riegger, Hal. *Primitive pottery.* New York, Van Nostrand Reinhold Co., 1972. 120 pp, ill.

Riegger, Hal. *Raku: art and technique.* New York, Van Nostrand Reinhold, 1970. 136 pp, many ill, biblio, index.

Schwartz, Marvin D., Reitz, Donald, Hendricks, Charles, and Pilcher, Donald. *Salt glaze ceramics.* New York, American Crafts Council, 1972. 36 pp, many ill.

Wildenhain, Marguerite. *Pottery: form and expression.* Palo Alto, California and New York, Pacific Books and American Crafts Council, reissued 1973. 157 pp, ill.

Wildenhain, Marguerite. *The invisible core: a potter's life and thought.* Palo Alto, California, Pacific Books, 1973. 207 pp, ill.

Wilkinson, Charles K. *Iranian ceramics.* New York, Asia House, 1963. iv, 145 pp, 99 ill, biblio.

Yoshida, Mitsukuni. *In search of Persian pottery.* New York, Weatherhill/Tankosha, 1972. vi, 161 pp, 108 ill.

Fiber

Albers, Anni. *On weaving.* Middletown, Conn., Wesleyan University, 1965. 204 pp, 121 ill.

Atwater, Mary Meigs. *Byways in hand-weaving.* New York, The Macmillan Co., 1972. 128 pp, 27 ill, 36 diagrams.

Bacon, Lenice Ingram. *American patchwork quilts.* New York, William Morrow Co., 1973. 190 pp, many ill, biblio, index.

Belfer, Nancy. *Designing in stitching and appliqué.* Worcester, Mass., Davis Publications, Inc., 1972. 128 pp, 8 color plates, ill.

Belfer, Nancy. *Designing in batik and tie dye.* Worcester, Mass., Davis Publications, Inc., 1972. 117 pp, ill.

Beutlich, Tadek. *The technique of woven tapestry.* London, B. T. Batsford, 1967. 128 pp, 134 ill, text figs, glossary, biblio, suppliers, index.

Bird, Junius. *Paracas fabrics and Nazca needlework 3rd century B.C.–3rd century A.D.* Washington, D.C., Textile Museum, 1954. 126 pp, 127 plates, maps, charts, biblio, index.

Black, Mary E. *New key to weaving: a textbook of hand weaving for the beginning weaver.* Milwaukee, Bruce, 1957. xv, 571 pp, 658 ill, glossary, standard sizes, biblio, index.

Bühler, Alfred. *Ikat, batik, plangi: reservemusterungen auf garn und stoff aus Vorderasien, Zentralasien, Südosteuropa und Nordafrika.* Basel, Pharos, Hansrudolf Schwabe, 1972. 3 volumes: Volume I xiv, 347 pp, text figs—historical and technical survey; Volume II 102 pp, biblio, tables, maps, index; Volume III 505 ill.

Bystrom, Ellen. *Printing on fabric: basic techniques.* New York, Van Nostrand Reinhold Co., 1971. 96 pp, many ill, text figs.

Collingwood, Peter. *The techniques of rug weaving.* London, Faber & Faber, 1968. 527 pp, 170 ill, text figs, biblio, suppliers, index. Also New York, Watson-Guptill, 1968.

Constantine, Mildred, and Larsen, Jack Lenor. *Beyond craft: the art fabric.* New York, Van Nostrand Reinhold, 1973. 288 pp, 260 ill, text figs.

Cyrus, Ulla. *Manual of Swedish hand weaving.* Boston, Charles T. Branford, 1956. 271 pp, 141 ill, glossary, index.

Davenport, Elsie G. *Yarn dyeing.* London, Sylvan, 1955. 127 pp, text figs.

Edson, Nicki Hitz, and Stimmel, Arlene. *Creative crochet.* New York, Watson-Guptill Publications, 1973. 143 pp, many ill, suppliers list, biblio, index.

Edwards, A. Cecil. *The Persian carpet: a survey of the carpet-weaving industry of Persia.* London, Gerald Duckworth, 1953. xvi, 384 pp, 423 ill, maps, appendices, index.

Emery. Irene. *The primary structures of fabrics: an illustrated classification.* Washington, D.C., The Textile Museum, 1966. 339 pp, many ill, 376 figures, glossary, biblio.

Enthoven, Jacqueline. *The stitches of creative embroidery.* New York, Reinhold Co., 1964. 212 pp, many ill, index of stitches.

Fannin, Allen. *Handspinning, art and technique.* New York, Reinhold Co., 1970. 208 pp, many ill, glossary, index.

Fél, Edit. *Hungarian peasant embroidery.* London, B.T. Batsford, 1961. 138 pp, 64 ill, text figs, index.

Forman, W. and B., and Wassef, Ramses Wissa. *Tapestries from Egypt woven by the children of Harrania.* London, Paul Hamlyn, c1968. 36 pp, 66 ill.

Graumont, Raoul and Hensel, John. *Encyclopedia of knots and fancy ropework.* Cambridge, Md., Cornell Maritime Press, 1958. 690 pp, 347 ill, glossary, index.

Groves, Sylvia. *The history of needlework tools and accessories.* London, Country Life, 1966. 136 pp, 199 ill, text figs, index.

Gutcheon, Beth. *The perfect patchwork primer.* New York, David McKay Co., 1973. 257 pp.

Hanley, Hope. *Needlepoint.* New York, Scribner and Sons, 1964. 156 pp, many ill, suppliers list, biblio, index of stitches.

Harvey, Virginia. *Macramé: the art of creative knotting.* New York, Reinhold Co., 1967. 128 pp, suppliers list, biblio, glossary.

Holstein, Jonathan. *The pieced quilt: an American design tradition.* Greenwich, Conn., New York Graphic Society, 1973. 192 pp, ill.

James, George Wharton. *Indian basketry,* and *How to make Indian and other baskets* (two volumes in one). Reprint edition New York, Dover Publications, Inc., 1972. 272 pp, 355 ill; 142 pp, 223 ill, biblio, index.

Johnston, Meda Parker, and Kaufman, Glen. *Design on fabrics.* New York, Reinhold Co., 1967. 155 pp, many ill, suppliers list, glossary, biblio, index.

Kaufmann, Ruth. *The new American tapestry.* New York, Reinhold Co., 1968. 104 pp, 50 ill.

Kooijman, Simon. *Tapa in Polynesia.* Honolulu, Bishop Museum, 1972. xiv, 498 pp, many ill, biblio.

Krevitsky, Nik. *Stitchery: art and craft.* New York, Reinhold Co., 1966. 132 pp, many ill, biblio.

Kuenzi, André. *La nouvelle tapisserie.* Geneva, les Editions de Bonvent, 1973. 303 pp, many ill.

Landreau, Anthony N., and Pickering, W. R. *From the Bosporus to Samarkand; flat-woven rugs.* Washington, D.C., The Textile Museum, 1969. 112 pp, 113 ill, biblio.

Laury, Jean Ray. *Doll making: a creative approach.* New York, Reinhold Co., 1970. 136 pp, 94 ill.

Lejard, Andre (ed). *French tapestry.* London, Paul Elek, 1946. 107 pp, 129 ill, biblio.

Lesch, Alma. *Vegetable dyeing.* New York, Watson-Guptill Publications, 1970. 146 pp, charts, suppliers list, biblio, index.

Lévi-Strauss, Monique. *Sheila Hicks.* Paris, Editions Pierre Horay, 1973. 80 pp, 130 ill.

Nordlund, Odd. *Primitive Scandinavian textiles in knotless netting.* Oslo, Oslo University Press, 1961. 154 pp, 82 ill, biblio.

Nye, Thelma (ed). *Swedish weaving.* New York, Van Nostrand Reinhold Co., 1972. 120 pp, ill.

Oakes, Alma, and Hill, Margot Hamilton. *Rural costume: its origin and development in Western Europe and the British Isles.* London, Batsford, 1970/New York, Reinhold Co. 248 pp, 378 ill, glossary, appendices, biblio, index.

Phillips, Mary Walker. *Creative knitting: a new art form.* New York, Van Nostrand Reinhold Co., 1971. 119 pp, 81 ill, biblio, index.

Regensteiner, Else. *The art of weaving.* New York, Reinhold Co., 1970. 184 pp, many ill, glossary, biblio, index.

Robertson, Seonaid M. *Dyes from plants.* New York, Van Nostrand Reinhold Co., 1973. 144 pp.

Rossbach, Ed. *Baskets as textile art.* New York, Van Nostrand Reinhold Co., 1973. 199 pp, 228 ill, biblio, index.

Roth, Ling. *Studies in primitive looms.* Halifax, Nova Scotia, Bankfield Museum, 1918. 154 pp, ill, index.

Schuette, Marie, and Müller-Christensen, Sigrid. *A pictorial history of embroidery.* New York, Frederick A. Praeger, 1964. xxiv, 336 pp, 464 ill, index.

Stapley, Mildred. *Popular weaving and embroidery in Spain.* New York, William Helburn, 1924. xii, 182 pp, 121 ill, text figs.

Thorpe, Azalea Stuart, and Larsen, Jack Lenor. *Elements of weaving.* New York, Doubleday and Co., 1967. 257 pp, 71 ill, text figs.

Waller, Irene. *Designing with thread—from fibre to fabric.* New York, Viking Press, 1973.

Glass

Amaya, Mario. *Tiffany glass.* New York, Walker and Co., 1967. 84 pp, many ill.

Anderson, Harriette. *Kiln-fired glass.* Philadelphia, Chilton, 1970. xv, 185 pp, 173 ill, glossary, biblio, suppliers, index.

Armitage, E. Liddall. *Stained glass: history, technology and practice.* London, Leonard Hill, Grampian Press, 1960. 216 pp, 117 ill, glossary, biblio.

Beard, Geoffrey. *Modern glass.* London, Studio Vista, 1968. 160 pp, 124 ill, biblio, index to illustrations.

Burton, John. *Glass: philosophy and method: handblown, sculptured, color.* Philadelphia, Chilton, 1967. 278 pp, 281 ill, biblio, index.

Harden, D. B., and others. *Masterpieces of glass.* London, British Museum, 1968. 199 pp, 269 ill, biblio.

Littleton, Harvey. *Glassblowing: a search for form.* New York, Van Nostrand Reinhold Co., 1971. 143 pp, many ill, glossary, biblio, index.

Mariacher, Giovanni. *Italian blown glass from ancient Rome to Venice.* New York, McGraw-Hill, 1961. 247 pp, 142 ill, biblio, index.

Middlemas, Keith. *Continental coloured glass.* London, Barrie & Jenkins, 1971. 120 pp, many ill.

Neustadt, Dr. Egon. *The lamps of Tiffany.* New York, The Fairfield Press (Barnes), 1970. 224 pp, 300+ plates (238 color), biblio.

Polak, Ada. *Modern glass.* London, Faber & Faber, 1962. 94 pp, 96 ill, biblio, index.

Reyntiens, Patrick. *The technique of stained glass.* New York, Watson-Guptill, 1967. 192 pp, 232 ill, glossary, biblio, index.

Schrijver, Elka. *Glass and crystal.* New York, Universe, 1964. 2 volumes: I from earliest times to 1850; II from 1850 to the present. Many ill, biblio, index.

Schuler, Frederic. *Flameworking: glassmaking for the craftsman.* Philadelphia, Chilton, 1968. xiv, 131 pp, many ill, appendices, suppliers.

Schuler, Frederic and Lilli. *Glassforming: glassmaking for the craftsman.* Philadelphia, Chilton, 1970. xv, 151 pp, 114 ill, appendices, suppliers, biblio, index.

Sowers, Robert. *Stained glass: an architectural art.* New York, Universe, 1965. 128 pp, 122 ill.

Stennet-Willson, R. *The Beauty of modern glass.* London, Studio, 1958. 128 pp, many ill.

Metal

Ball, Fred. *Experimental techniques in enameling.* New York, Van Nostrand Reinhold Co., 1972. 144 pp, ill.

Barsali, Isa Belli. *European enamels.* London, Paul Hamlyn, 1966. 158 pp, 71 ill.

Benda, Klement. *Ornament and jewellery: archaeological finds from Eastern Europe.* Prague, Artia, 1967. 113 pp, 88 ill, notes.

Besancenot, Jean. *Bijoux arabes et berbères du Maroc.* Casablanca, de la Cigogne, 1953. xv, 18 pp, 40 ill, biblio.

Brijbhushusan, Jamila. *Indian jewellery, ornaments and decorative designs.* Bombay, D. P. Taraporevala, 1964. 2nd revised edition. 82 ill, text figs, appendices, biblio, index.

Charron, Shirley. *Modern pewter.* New York, Van Nostrand Reinhold Co., 1973. 142 pp.

Council for Small Industries in Rural Areas. *The blacksmith's craft: an introduction to blacksmithing for apprentices and craftsmen.* London, COSIRA, 1952. xii, 104 pp, 258 ill, biblio.

Davis, Mary L., and Pack, Greta. *Mexican jewelry.* Austin, University of Texas, 1963. xvi, 262 pp, 145 ill, biblio, index.

Gerlach, Martin (ed). *Primitive and folk jewelry.* Introduction and captions by Michael Haberlandt. New York, Dover, 1971. xvi, 219 pp, 109 ill.

Hiort, Esbjorn. *Modern Danish silver: Argenterie moderne danoise: Modern dänische Silberkunst: Modern Dansk solv.* New York, Museum/London, A. Zwemmer/Stuttgart, Gerd Hatje/Teufers, Arthur Niggli/Kobenhavn, Jul. Gjellerups, 1954. 124 pp, many ill, index. Multilingual text.

Hughes, Graham. *The art of jewelry*. New York, Viking Press, 1972. 248 pp, many ill, biblio, index.

Hughes, Graham. *Modern jewelry: an international survey 1890-1963*. London, Studio, 1963. 256 pp, 415 ill, biographies, biblio.

Hughes, Graham. *Modern silver throughout the world 1880-1967*. London, Studio Vista, 1967. 256 pp, 480 ill, biographies, biblio, index.

Kerfoot, J. B. *American pewter*. New York, Crown Publishers, 1942. 236 pp, 358 ill, index.

Kühn, Fritz. *Wrought iron*. London, Harrap, 1965. 120 pp, many ill.

Maryon, Herbert. *Metalwork and enamelling: a practical treatise on gold and silversmiths' work and their allied crafts*. London, Chapman & Hall, 1912. xiii, 327 pp, 383 ill, notes, biblio, index.

Morton, Philip. *Contemporary jewelry: a studio handbook*. New York, Holt, Rinehart and Winston, 1970. xii, 308 pp, 438 ill, biblio, index.

Plass, Margaret Webster. *African miniatures: the goldweights of the Ashanti*. London, Lund Humphries, 1967. 26 pp, 166 ill, biblio, map, classification.

Ricketts, Howard. *Objects of vertu*. London, Barrie & Jenkins, 1971. 124 pp, many ill, biblio, index. Published in the United States as "Antique gold and enamelware in color".

Roth, H. Ling. *Oriental silverwork: Malay and Chinese: a handbook for connoisseurs, collectors, students and silversmiths*. London, Truslove and Hanson, 1910. viii, 300 pp, 171 ill, text figs, index.

Seeler, Margarete. *The art of enameling: how to shape precious metal and decorate it with cloisonné, champlevé, plique-à-jour, mercury gilding and other fine techniques*. New York, Reinhold Co., 1969. 128 pp, many ill, index.

Smith, Cyril Stanley. *A history of metallography: development of ideas on the structure of metals before 1890*. Chicago, University of Chicago Press, 1960. 291 pp, 110 ill, appendices, biblio, index.

Untracht, Oppi. *Enameling on metal*. Philadelphia, Chilton, 1957. 191 pp, many ill, tables, biblio, index.

Untracht, Oppi. *Metal techniques for craftsmen: a basic manual for craftsmen on the methods of forming and decorating metals*. New York, Doubleday, 1968. xiv, 509 pp, many ill, suppliers, glossary, biblio, index.

Von Neumann, Robert. *The design and creation of jewelry*. New York, Chilton, 1961. xii, 271 pp, many ill, biblio, suppliers, appendices, index.

Wood

Adams, Jeanette, and Stieri, E. *The complete woodworking handbook*. New York, Arco, 1960. 561 pp, 900 ill.

Albarda, Jan H. *Wood, wire and quill: an introduction to the harpsichord*. Toronto, The Coach House, 1968. 96 pp, 12 ill, text figs, glossary, selection of music, index.

Andrews, Edward Deming, and Andrews, Faith. *Shaker furniture: the craftsmanship of an American communal sect*. New York, Dover Publications, 1950. 88 pp, 40 ill.

Austin, Robert, and Ueda, Koichiro. *Bamboo*. New York and Tokyo, Walker/Weatherhill, 1970. 215 pp, many ill, biblio.

Edlin, H. L. *Woodland crafts in Britain: an account of the traditional uses of trees and timbers in the British countryside*. London, B. T. Batsford, 1949. x, 182 pp, 159 ill, index.

Fagg, William. *Miniature wood carvings of Africa*. Bath, Adams & Dart, 1970. 104 pp, 90 ill, biblio.

Lincoln, William Alexander. *The art and practice of marquetry*. London, Thames & Hudson, 1971. 303 pp, 180 ill, appendices, index.

McDonnell, Leo P., Kidd, Donald M., and Sly, Louis J. *Hand wood working tools*. New York, Delmar, 1962. viii, 294 pp, many ill, index.

Moody, Ella. *Modern furniture*. New York, London, Dutton/Studio Vista, 1966. 160 pp, many ill, biblio.

Pinto, Edward H. *Treen and other wooden bygones: an encyclopaedia and social history*. London, George Bell & Sons, 1969. x, 458 pp, 460 ill, text figs, appendices, biblio, glossary, index.

Röttger, Ernst. *Creative wood design*. New York, Reinhold Co., 1961. 96 pp, 244 ill. Published in the United Kingdom as "Creative wood craft", B. T. Batsford.

Simpson, Thomas. *Fantasy furniture: design and decoration*. New York, Reinhold Co., 1968. 95 pp, many ill.

Sloane, Irving. *Classic guitar construction*. New York, Dutton, 1967. 95 pp, 130 ill.

Other Media

Antreasian, Garo Z., and Adams, Clinton. *The Tamarind book of lithography: art and techniques*. Los Angeles, New York, Tamarind Lithography Workshops/Harry N. Abrams, 1971. 464 pp, many ill, text figs, biblio, index.

Ashton, Dore, Campbell, Lawrence, and others (texts). *The mosaics of Jeanne Reynal*. New York, George Wittenborn, 1964. 111 pp, many ill, biblio.

Beaumont, Cyril W. *Puppets and the puppet stage*. London, The Studio, 1938. 32 pp, 144 ill.

Biegeleisen, J. I. *Screen printing: a contemporary guide to the technique of screen printing for artists, designers and craftsmen*. New York, Watson-Guptill, 1971. 159 pp, many ill, glossary, suppliers, biblio, index.

Catich, Edward M. *The origin of the serif. Brush writing and Roman letters*. Davenport, Iowa, The Catfish Press, 1968. xii, 310 pp, many ill, notes, index.

Cockerell, Douglas. *Bookbinding and the care of books: a textbook for bookbinders and librarians*. London, Sir Isaac Pitman, 1925. xvi, 333 pp, 8 ill, text figs, specifications, glossary, index.

Diehl, Edith. *Bookbinding: its background and technique*. New York, Rinehart, 1946. 2 volumes: xxi, 251 pp, 91 ill; vi, 406 pp, 189 figs, biblio, glossary, index.

Fischer, Peter. *Mosaic: history and technique.* London, Thames and Hudson, 1971. 152 pp, 120 ill, text figs, biblio, index.

Fox, Carl. *The doll.* New York, Harry N. Abrams, 1972. 343 pp, 191 ill, biblio.

Gall, G. *Leder im europäischen kunsthandwerk: ein handbuch für sammler und liebhaber.* Braunschweig, Klinkhardt u. Biermann, 1965. xii, 406 pp, 320 ill.

Honda, Isao. *The world of origami.* Tokyo, Japan Publications, 1965. 264 pp, many ill, biblio, index of folds.

Hunter, Dard. *Papermaking: the history and technique of an ancient craft.* New York, Knopf, 1943. xvi, 398 pp, 163 ill, biblio, notes, index.

Huth, Hans. *Lacquer of the west: the history of a craft and an industry, 1550-1850.* Chicago, University of Chicago, 1971. x, 158 pp, 364 ill, biblio, index.

Jahss, Melvin and Betty. *Inro and other miniature forms of Japanese lacquer art.* Rutland, Vermont, Charles E. Tuttle, 1971. 488 pp, 245 ill, list of artists, genealogical charts, glossary, biblio, index.

Lamb, C. M. (ed). *The calligrapher's handbook.* London, Faber & Faber, 1968. 253 pp, 50 ill, text figs, appendices, biblio, index.

Lambeth, M. *The golden dolly: the art, mystery and history of corn dollies through the ages, describing all types and how to make them.* Fulbourn, UK, Cornucopia, 1963. 92 pp, 27 ill, text figs.

Lee Yu-Kuan. *Oriental lacquer art.* New York, Weatherhill, 1972. 394 pp, 264 ill, chronology, biblio, appendices.

Loring, Rosamond B. *Decorated book papers: being an account of their designs and fashions.* Second edition edited by Philip Hofer. Cambridge, Harvard University, 1952. xxxvi, 171 pp, 16 ill, appendices, notes, index.

Neal, Avon. *Ephemeral folk figures: scarecrows, harvest figures and snowmen.* New York, Clarkson N. Potter, 1969. 176 pp, 125 ill.

Newman, Thelma. *Plastics as design form.* Philadelphia, Chilton, 1972. 349 pp, many ill, appendices, glossary, biblio, index.

Orchard, William C. *The technique of porcupine quill decoration among the Indians of North America.* New York, Museum of the American Indian Heye Foundation, 1971. 85 pp, 30 ill, text figs.

Pettit, Florence H. *How to make whirligigs and whimmydiddles and other American folkcraft objects.* New York, Thomas Y. Crowell, 1972. xvi, 349 pp, many ill, glossary, biblio, index.

Sakamoto, Kazuya. *Japanese toys: playing with history.* Tokyo, Bijitsu Shuppan-Sha and Charles E. Tuttle, 1965. 516 pp, 394 ill, index.

Scott-Kemball, Jeune. *Javanese shadow puppets: the Raffles collection in the British Museum.* London, The British Museum, 1970. 65 pp, 30 ill, glossary, biblio, index.

Small, Claude. *Creative plastics techniques.* New York, Van Nostrand Reinhold Co., 1973. 124 pp, ill.

Stribling, Mary Lou. *Mosaic techniques: new aspects in fragmented design.* New York, Crown Publishers, 1966. 244 pp, 443 ill, appendices, glossary, suppliers list, biblio, index.

Waterer, John W. *Leather craftsmanship.* London, George Bell & Sons, 1968. 121 pp, 129 ill, biblio, glossary, index. Note: not the same book as this author's earlier *Leather and craftsmanship.*

Yamada, Sadami, and Ito, Kiyotado. *New dimensions in paper craft.* New York, Japan Publications, 1966. 264 pp, 600 ill, text figs.

Photographic Credits

With the exception of those noted below, all photographs are by Little Bobby Hanson, New York.

1, 10, 15, 52, 61, 65, 85, 123, 124, 147, 172 National Film Board of Canada
2, 11 Larry Burrows, Time-Life Picture Agency
3, 17, 142 Dr. Pascal James Imperato, New York
4, 5, 6, 7, 8, 76, 167, 168, 173 George Holton, New York
9 Courtesy of Landsforbundet Norsk Brukskunst, Oslo
18 Courtesy of Margaret M. Patch, World Crafts Council, New York
26 Courtesy of Agrupación de Actividades Artesanas del FAD, Barcelona
44 Stanley Lechtzin, Philadelphia
53 Gayle Wimmer, New York
63 Hal Babitt, California, with the assistance of Daniel Cobblah, Accra, Ghana
127, 170 Courtesy of Japan National Tourist Organization, New York

146 Courtesy of Crafts Advisory Committee, London
154, 171 Courtesy of Ministry of Education and Culture, Djakarta
157 Courtesy of Swiss National Tourist Office, New York
169, 174 John Reader, Time-Life Picture Agency
180 Courtesy of Johnson Wax, Racine, Wisconsin
185 Courtesy of Craft Horizons, American Crafts Council, New York
193 Renita Hanfling; photograph courtesy of Peter Voulkos
205 Sten Robért, Sweden
216 Courtesy of Wendy Ramshaw, London
217 Chris Baker, London

The photographs provided by the National Film Board of Canada are taken from the film In Praise of Hands, produced by the National Film Board in association with the Province of Ontario and the World Crafts Council, 1974.

Contributing National Organizations

Australia	Crafts Council of Australia	**Netherlands**	Centraal Orgaan voor het Scheppend Ambacht (C.O.S.A.); Netherlands Art Foundation; Plastic Art Section, Ministry of Culture, Welfare, and Social Work
Austria	Austrian Crafts Council		
Canada	Canadian Guild of Crafts (Ontario); Canadian Committee of the World Crafts Council		
		New Hebrides	Résidence de France
Colombia	PROARTE	**New Zealand**	New Zealand Crafts Council, Inc.
Cyprus	Folk Art Association	**Nigeria**	Nigerian Arts Council
Czechoslovakia	Ustredie Umeleckých Remesiel	**Norway**	Landsforbundet Norsk Brukskunst
Denmark	The Danish Society of Arts and Crafts and Industrial Design	**Papua New Guinea**	Papua New Guinea Public Museum and Art Gallery
Ecuador	Centro de Diseño y Artesanía	**Peru**	Asociación Nacional de Artesanos
Ethiopia	National Museum	**Poland**	CEPELIA
Finland	ORNAMO	**Senegal**	Office Sénégalais de l'artisanat
France	Association Française des Métiers d'Art et de Création; Maison des Métiers d'Art	**Sierra Leone**	Ministry of Trade and Industry
		Spain	Agrupación de Actividades Artesanas del FAD
Germany	Arbeitsgemeinschaft des deutschen Kunsthandwerks	**Sweden**	Svenska Slöjdföreningen
		Switzerland	WCC Swiss Section; Cultural Division, Federal Department of the Interior
Ghana	National Association of Craftsmen		
Greece	WCC Greek Section	**Togo**	La Division de l'Artisanat, Secrétariat d'Etat Chargé du Commerce, de l'Industrie et du Plan
Hungary	Iparmüvészeti Vállalat		
Iceland	Iceland Handcrafts Association		
India	Crafts Council of India; All India Handicrafts Board	**United Kingdom**	International Committee of the British Crafts Centre; The Crafts Advisory Committee
Indonesia	Fine Art Division, Ministry of Education and Culture	**United States**	American Crafts Council, International Department
Iran	Iranian Handicrafts Centre	**Venezuela**	WCC Venezuelan Section
Ireland	Crafts Council of Ireland		
Israel	Israel Designer-Craftsmen's Association		
Italy	WCC Sezione Italiana	**Cameroon**	Special thanks are rendered to the Agence de Coopération Culturelle et Technique, Paris, and to the Director of its Montreal office, M. Paul Bouvrette, for making it possible to include in the Exhibition outstanding examples of the crafts of these countries.
Japan	Japan Foundation	**Chad**	
Jordan	Jordan Crafts Council	**Dahomey**	
Korea	Korea Design and Packaging Center	**Ivory Coast**	
Lebanon	Maison de l'Artisan Libanais; Ministry of Information	**Mali**	
		Niger	
Liberia	Liberian Arts and Crafts Association	**Rwanda**	
Malta	Malta Crafts Centre	**Senegal**	
Mexico	Comité Méxicano Pro Artesanías y Artes Populares	**Togo**	

In addition to the national organizations listed above, the World Crafts Council expresses its sincere appreciation to the following individuals and organizations who have rendered invaluable assistance in the creation of this book:

Staff members of the American Crafts Council
Lois Moran, Joanne Polster, Reba Wertentheil and the entire staff of the Research and Education Department; Barbara Bullock, Maureen Herbert, Diana Penzner, Mimi Pichey, and Doris Stowens.

Individuals
Glenda Arentzen, New York
Françoise Grossen, New York
Lo Holton, New York
Dr. Pascal James Imperato, New York
Mel Someroski, Kent, Ohio
Milton Sonday, New York
Byron Temple, Lambertville, New Jersey

Shops, Galleries and Companies
André Emmerich Gallery, New York
Capricorn, Colombo, Sri Lanka
Eastman Kodak Company, Rochester, New York
Go Fly A Kite, New York
India Nepal Shop, New York
Keshav's Crafts, Kathmandu, Nepal
Tribal Arts Gallery, New York
United Nations Gift Centre, New York, Director June Henneberger and staff

International Organizations
Afro-Art, Stockholm
World Council of Churches, Geneva, Nina Lengyel, Analyst for Technical Projects

Index of Countries

Index of Craftsmen